I0467954

DISCOVERING GROWTH STOCKS AND ANTICIPATING PARABOLIC MOVES

RICHARD J. FRUTH

ISBN-13: 978-1500240561

The author and publisher have provided this e-book to you for your personal use only. You may not make this e-book publicly available in any way. Copyright infringement is against the law. If you believe the copy of this e-book you are reading infringes on the author's copyright, please notify our publisher at james@rjfruth.com

©2014 Richard J. Fruth

Contents

INTRODUCTION

This book was first started over 35 years ago. Strange it may seem that only now has it been completed. The investment philosophy described herein has been successfully proven and is even more valuable today. It would be most unfortunate if the knowledge attained was not shared, passed on to future market participants to enhance their market performance. The catalyst to finish this work was a request to speak at the 2011 Spring Conference of the American Associates of Professional Technical Analysts in Marina del Rey, California. The title of my presentation was "The Art of Anticipation, How to Anticipate Parabolic moves in Stock Prices Through Analysis of Diminishing Float." The talk was well received and I was strongly encouraged to finish the book.

Two themes are central to this work. The first is understanding the importance of supply and demand in moving stock prices. Although this may seem very basic, few market participants fully grasp the concept or for that matter how to read the signs of accumulation and distribution. Secondly, that technical analysis is not just a short term trading tool, but can be a powerful long term investment tool. Being able to anticipate price moves in a stock, that doubles, triples or more is not only obviously rewarding, but just plain fun. This art has almost been lost because of a momentous change that took place in the brokerage industry.

May 1, 1975 or Mayday as it was referred to, marked the end of fixed commission rates and the new era of negotiated brokerage charges. Prior to that date brokerage commission rates were very high and it could cost in some cases almost a full point, i.e. a dollar a share to buy or sell a stock. Further the rate per share was almost the same for a 1000 share trade as a 100 share buy or sell. Day trading was impossible. Today you can trade 100 shares or a thousand shares for less than $10 total. If you are an active trader, trading thousands of shares, rates for high frequency trades can be even lower.

Discovering Growth Stocks and Anticipating Parabolic Moves

The importance of this can be seen when prior to 1975 the brokerage industry consisted of two separate areas. The very lucrative institutional business serviced the mutual fund industry, insurance companies and other buyers of large quantities of common stock. Small research boutique brokerage firms flourished on the exorbitant commissions received. The other area, known as the retail side of the business served the individual investor. The end of fixed rates resulted in dramatic declines in commissions to the institutional client. Many of the small boutique firms serving them were forced to merge with larger organizations or leave the business. Meanwhile, the retail brokerage firms, those who served the individual investor, had to find other sources of revenue. They expanded their product offerings to include the sale of mutual funds, limited partnerships, tax shelters, insurance, put and call options and any other financial product imaginable. The traditional stockbroker, who knew and studied individual companies, was quickly replaced by well-trained salespeople who could explain the features and benefits of a multitude of products.

Today an investor can buy and sell a stock profitably after commissions with a move in price of less than a dollar. Before Mayday it would have taken a price move of over a full point. Of course rates for the retail client dropped gradually, but lower commissions resulted in an explosion in trading volume. It's hard to believe that in the early 1970's trading volume on the New York Stock Exchange averaged 3 million shares a day. Today, billion share days are common. Speculation, day trading has become the pastime for millions of people. Just because you can actively trade doesn't mean it's right for everyone. Some individuals neither have the time nor the temperament for short term trading. Although the idea of actively trading has the allure of getting rich quick, for many the results are painfully disappointing.

Significant long term gains are not only possible but make sense for those individuals who have wealth and want to see it continue to grow without undue risk. For those who have not yet attained wealth, I would certainly encourage building a portfolio of great growth stocks. This book will show you how to accomplish that goal. For those fortunate enough to have amassed a large estate, this should prove to be an excellent guide to help protect and grow their wealth. Finally, the professional money manager will find encouragement and guidance in stock selection and account management.

Many of my contemporaries look at this approach as old fashioned, that technical analysis was meant to be for short term trading, not long term investing, but at the end of the day it's who has the most success that counts. I have lived the stock market for well over the past forty years. First as a retail broker, on the sell side of the business, making a living from commissions. The past 20 years have been far more enjoyable for me and rewarding for my clients on the buy side of the business, as a fee only manager of common stock portfolios.

ACKNOWLEDGEMENTS

I would first like to thank all my friends that I have had the good fortune to meet through the Market Technicians Association, The American Association of Professional Technical Analysts and The International Association of Technical Analyst. These are great organizations and provide a wonderful venue for meeting and sharing ideas and experiences.

Special thanks to Peter Mauthe who has given me the extra push to get this book finished. Also, Dave Landry who's advice and critique has been invaluable. Miss Lindsay Graham has been a big help to an engineer that sometimes needs help with grammar as well as basic computer skills. Nino Rinaldi who has generously given us numerous charts shown in this book. Thanks to Dick Arms, Larry McMillan, Greg Morris and Walter Deemer for their advice and counsel. Although John Brooks and John Magee are no longer with us they have played an important part in my growth and knowledge. I appreciate the kindness and warmth of the entire technical analysis community.

ACKNOWLEDGMENT

PART I

A parabolic stock move is a chart pattern in which price rises with an increasingly steeper slope. Where time is the enemy and the advance reaches a terminal velocity, at which point the price advance slows, fails to advance and then reverses in a dramatic decline.

CHAPTER ONE

THE MENTOR AND HIS GIFT TO ME

It was sometime in the early 1970s when I first discovered what would prove to be a most important insight explaining what causes stock prices to advance. I want to share this with any serious investor who wants to know what really moves stock prices and how to discover the great growth stocks and anticipate potential parabolic moves.

A brief paragraph of my background will help explain what led me to the mentor who helped show me the light. I bought my first stock, 10 shares of Toledo Edison, at the age of 12 and by the age 16 was trying to absorb Edwards and Magee's book *Technical Analysis of Stock Trends.* Charting stocks was part of my daily routine at Michigan State University, where I earned a degree in Chemical Engineering, which is what brought me to Houston, Texas. But the market was my passion, and I soon gave up a very comfortable position in the chemical industry to become a technical analyst. I went to every investment firm in the area looking for work, but to no avail. I will never forget one interview I had with the head of the investment department of a large insurance company; I sat across the desk from an old curmudgeon who said, "Boy, you decide what to buy and sell based on those squiggles on a chart?" I replied, "Yes sir, I do." His quick response was, "not here, you don't."

The only entry for me into the business was to become a stockbroker, a position which I reluctantly accepted. Houston was far away from my hometown in Ohio where I had grown up. It was difficult in the early 1970's to build a business from scratch where nobody knew you. In those days, brokerage offices had several rows of theater seats in the rear of the office where customers could sit and watch the tape and place their trades. The Trans-Lux tape that moved continually across the wall, displaying the changing price action was quite an advancement. These folks, mainly men sitting in the back of the room, were derogatorily referred to by the other brokers as *squatters*. They were looked upon as retired folks who needed some place to go and not a good source of business. But I was desperate to find business anywhere I could, and I was kind to these folks. To my good fortune a number of them opened accounts with me and I did pick up some business. One of the fellows, a retired tool and die maker, took a liking to me and explained that he would like to have me handle his account. I believe he had suffered from a slight stroke because his speech was impaired, and he explained with some difficulty that he would trade very infrequently but that it would be worthwhile. Many months went by without a trade. Then one day he came in, took out an envelope that contained several thousand shares of common stock. I don't remember the name of the stock, but in those days many investors *took delivery* of their stock certificates rather than trust a brokerage firm to hold their shares. Those were the days before SIPC Insurance[i]. The stock had gone on a significant run and he felt it was time to take his profit and run. I was very happy for him and very happy for myself. In those days before negotiated commissions, a sale of several thousand shares of stock would yield a commission of several hundred dollars. A week or so later when the trade settled he came into the office and had a list of three stocks he wanted to buy. The names of those stocks I don't recall, but I do remember that they were real *dogs*. I advised him not to buy these. They were not a good place for his money, and my firm's research could do much better for him. He smiled and shook his head no; this is what he wanted to do. I started to argue with him and then realized that I should shut up and be grateful for the commissions from three large trades. He then went on with some speech difficulty explaining that he bought what he called *tombstones*. He sketched out on a piece of paper the price action of a company that has a large rise and then a steep decline and then goes sideways for a very long time. He then explained that the stock would again have a very sharp rise again before another very dramatic decline and on a long term price chart they would look like tombstones.

I listened politely and placed his orders. I did not realize than that I had been given the genesis of what would become a life changing insight that would span over 40 years of stock market success. I would be able to interpret the price action of an individual stock, anticipate its movement, and see the cues of the beginning of a powerful advance. Although the process is very easy to understand, it took me a long time to fully appreciate all the ramifications of what had been revealed. Sometime later I came to realize my tool and die maker was a wealthy man. He had been in the stock market many years and knew far more about the market than anyone else I had ever met.

I believe most people are frustrated with their returns from bonds, real estate, and common stocks. They are finished with speculation, gambling with their life savings, retirement money and are looking for a well thought out approach to investing. Hopefully, this book will take the mystery out of wealth creation and enable the reader to learn how to efficiently identify common stocks with large long term capital gain potential and how to reduce risk while building wealth. It is a logical reasoned approach that is easy to understand and that any serious investor can implement. This straightforward understanding of the market is based on quickly grasping what makes a stock move. It is not for the speculator or day trader. A detailed analysis of one price chart will reveal the forces at work, taking the mystique out of fundamental and technical analysis.

---

[i] Securities Investor Protection Corporation

CHAPTER TWO

THE DISCOVERY

It was quite by accident, while leafing through *Moody's Handbook of Stocks* that I came across the write-up for a company called AMF Incorporated. At the top of the page was a 20 year chart of the price history of the stock and below a brief summary of the company. What caught my eye was the rapid advance in the price of the stock in the early 1960s and the subsequent price decline which was then followed by seven years of dull sideways action. Then again the stock had a rapid advance which again was followed by a subsequent dramatic decline. These two parabolic moves reminded me of the chart that my client, the tool and die maker, had sketched out on a piece of paper and called tombstones.

That a common stock would rise gradually from the mid-teens and then accelerate to over $60 a share I found very intriguing. And then, decline over the following year back to 10 was equally as amazing. Why did this happen? And then again, almost 10 years later AMF rose from the mid-teens well into the high 70s and then again declined to under $10 three years later. I was intrigued by what I saw and had to know what happened to cause the stock to behave in such a manner. Figure 2.1 shows this 20 year history of the price action of AMF Incorporated, a major manufacturer of bowling equipment. The rapid advance and subsequent decline are explained by the bowling craze that was then spreading across the United States. Bowling was the rage and the stock price soared as if there was no end to its advance, but as with any fad, the boom was followed quickly by a bust as the market for bowling equipment became saturated.

These are the fundamental reasons for the rise and fall of the stock. But more interesting is the analysis of the next 12 years' behavior. Understanding AMF's fundamentals during this period is important in order to fully appreciate the overriding influence of less obvious technical factors. A look at the earnings of AMF from 1964 to 1970 (figure 2.1) shows that earnings were increasing every year. That's real growth. AMF was steadily improving, diversifying into other areas and fundamentally becoming a vastly improved company. Strong enough to continue paying a high dividend even as the price languished at less than a small fraction of its 1961 peak. Throughout the exuberant markets of the 1960's, AMF's price performance was dull and it had become what Wall Street calls a *dog*.

Why was the stock so ignored in view of such obvious and dramatically improved fundamentals? Because so many shareholders were underwater, and the stock was trading far below their cost. This stock was under continual liquidation for 10 years. Those poor unfortunates who bought the stock during the latter part of its spectacular rise or more likely during its equally dramatic collapse when they thought they were being given a second chance to buy cheap or maybe averaging down, were now selling. They were succumbing, capitulating, and giving up hope, pitching out there shares, taking their licking.

You can see this by the fact that the stock was at its low point for the year in the fourth quarters of 1961, 1962, 1963, 1966 and 1967. Tax loss selling is predominant in the last quarter of any given year. Those who own a stock at higher prices have an excuse, a reason they will tell you, for disposing of their shares in order to establish a tax loss and salvage something from their debacle. Normal human behavior holds out hope that a stock will move higher but as the year end approaches the holder of AMF shares realizes that time is running out and he dumps his stock on the market, pushing the price down and in turn discouraging others. This supply coming on the market is a function of the calendar, year-end tax selling and has nothing to do with the fundamentals of the company. As a matter of fact, a careful look at the price performance of the stock shows a nice short term advance in each of the following Januaries. This is called understandably, the *January effect* and results from the absence of supply after the first of the year. Rare is the individual who takes a tax loss after year end.

Careful analysis of this chart reveals much more; look back to the sharp decline in 1961. The rapid decline wasn't caused by poor earnings announcements. After all, 1961 was a peak year in the earnings at that point, $1.70 per share. These results were for the year and weren't released until early 1962. Why did the stock price break down while earnings were still rising? The early part of the decline was the result of intelligent investors taking their profit and running. They realized that the earnings growth was not sustainable. That the stock was selling at 36 times earnings more than discounted any future potential. Most importantly, they realized that parabolic price moves are unsustainable and when the advance stops, the decline can be very dramatic.

Once the stock had peaked and started to decline, margin calls became a factor. Margin requirements in 1961 were 70%; in other words the buyer of 100 shares at $60 had to put up 70% of $6,000 or $4,200. A maintenance call for more funds would have been issued by his broker as his equity declined. Note the steep decline between a $50 and $30 on the chart. This was due to forced liquidation. Margin accounts were dumping their shares instead of meeting maintenance calls with more cash or possibly not being able to put up more money and having no choice but to sell. This liquidation feeds on itself. As margin selling drives down the stock, new margin calls are generated with each successive drop in the price of the stock. Supply overwhelms demand. A dynamic decline is in place which, in this case, finally climaxed in 1962, coincidentally with the low point for the market in general. At this point the stock in the very weakest of hands has been sold.

Now the laborious task of distribution and re-accumulation begins. Tax selling, frustrated stockholders seeing other stocks climb while theirs languishes, new buyers growing restless, as well as all sellers, are all part of the distribution process. Accumulation begins, starting with a new group of investors with different objectives. They are not the speculator, the margin buyer, or the *hot money* momentum stock player. Rather the buying comes from employee stock purchases, cautious stable investment by income oriented investors attracted by the generous 5% dividend yield and corporate buybacks of their own stock. Even the bowling enthusiasts buy the stock. This is a different shareowner than those who were part of the parabolic move. Gradually the stock falls into the hands of buyers who are content to hold their shares. This is accumulation.

One special nuance that sometimes occurs can be seen on the AMF chart, when the stock made a strong recovery high in December 1968. The stock reached a level approaching $30 in December which indicated the tax loss sellers were no longer a factor in the distribution process. This new recovery high represented an almost 50% advance over prices that prevailed during the preceding six years. That was enough gain to bring out the sellers, and the supply took the stock lower over the next eighteen months. A 50% gain at that time was impressive for such a laggard and cleaned out any remaining liquidity.

It could be argued that only a fool would own this stock at this point, but distribution is a fascinating process and for whatever reason, the amount of stock available to trade was gone; the stock is now tightly held. A similar rally can be seen in the Brunswick chart in 1969. This final rally and decline is the last gasp which cleans out the last speculator and sets up the tight supply situation necessary for a parabolic rise. It isn't necessary to always have this anomaly but it occurs more often than not.

By the early 1970s, the distribution accumulation process is complete and the stock is becoming scarce, meaning the float has thinned out, i.e. there is less stock available now to purchase and earnings are now growing more rapidly, fueled by of all things, a bowling boom in Japan. The stock easily advances to 67 1/4 by early 1972 from less than $20 in 1970. How fast we forget. The boom turns to bust just before the stock declines, this time with added momentum from the 1973-1974 bear market to just under $10 in 1974. The only other manufacturer of bowling equipment is Brunswick Corporation, and its chart is shown in figure 2.2. Same story, same lesson.

Careful analysis of the chart reveals the boom and bust cycle: supply and demand, distribution and accumulation, and the dynamics of the market. Understanding what the chart is telling you is the key to technical analysis. It is amazing that a stock at one point can trade at $10 a share and a year later trade at six times that price and then a year later be back to $10. Did the fundamentals improve that much and then deteriorate that much in such a short period of time? No. Human behavior, fear and greed drive stock prices. Deciphering when a stock is going through distribution is important in understanding underperformance of a common stock even during periods of improving fundamentals. Patiently observing the accumulation process, revealing the absorption of stock into strong hands is key to gaining an advantage where one can also participate in the accumulation process by buying common stocks when they are undervalued and then enjoying a dramatic rise to a point where they are excessively overvalued. It is at that point when the price is at its peak that Wall Street has fallen in love with the stock. There is much written about it in the press, and the stock is widely ballyhooed as having a great future. Brokerage firms issue glowing *research reports* with no reference to Graham & Dodd[ii] valuation analysis but rather quarterly earnings projections. The key is to anticipate the rise before it happens and also to anticipate the decline that will follow when the fools march in.

I have seen this pattern play out many times. What is so exciting about this drama is that it not only continues to repeat itself over and over, but that it challenges the skill and emotions of the best investor. After all, an investor who accumulates a stock at $10 and then watches it fluctuate in a narrow range must have patience. Then when the stock dramatically rises, doubles, triples in a short period of time he has to deal with a totally different set of emotions. The temptation here is to sell too soon. Many good technical tools can guide an investor as to when to sell. The parabolic price move can be the most rewarding pattern but it is also the most challenging and requires a great deal of self-control. It is very disheartening to round-trip a stock i.e. to ride it up and ride it down. The legendary investor and economist, John Maynard Keynes observed that the individual investor's success or failure was not influenced by intelligence or special information but rather by temperament. More to the point, this means how he behaved at market tops and bottoms. Buying into popular manias, price spikes and selling then cheap assets at or near stock lows is devastating to long term performance. So how do you know when a stock is over-priced or undervalued? Look again at the chart of AMF, it speaks reams of information. You don't want to be a member of the *buy high, sell low club*.

Not all stocks have parabolic moves, but enough do that an understanding of what is taking place is basic to understanding the forces at play in the market. It was fortunate that I came to appreciate the insight given me, not by an expert with titles and initials after his name, but rather by a tool and die maker with years of experience in the market. Whether you ever enjoy a parabolic move or not, the important insight is to realize what causes a stock to advance or decline. Once you master that, you will be in control of your financial success.

The single most important lesson to be learned from this chart is that the price action of a stock is determined by supply and demand. I can remember during a fairly tumultuous period when clients would call and say, "Why did the stock market decline today?" We were expected to have some intelligent sounding response explaining that something happened in Washington or something happened in the weather or what have you. The real answer would have been unacceptable but true, "there were more sellers than buyers". The market had to decline to where supply and demand came into balance. The same is true in an advancing market. When you begin to think of the stock market as a place of price discovery where supply and demand find a balance, then you will become free of the noise, emotion, and banter of those who chatter about quarterly earnings and other drivel. People buy and sell; they collectively make up the supply-demand equation. For those who don't believe in supply and demand, who refuse to recognize technical analysis, I am reminded when in earlier times a similar group of fools believed the earth was flat.

[ii] Graham and Dodd strongly expressed the view that common stocks can be evaluated based on such measurements as cash flow, debt to equity ratios, management etc. They would be horrified by today's obsession with quarterly earnings in place of sound balance sheet analysis.

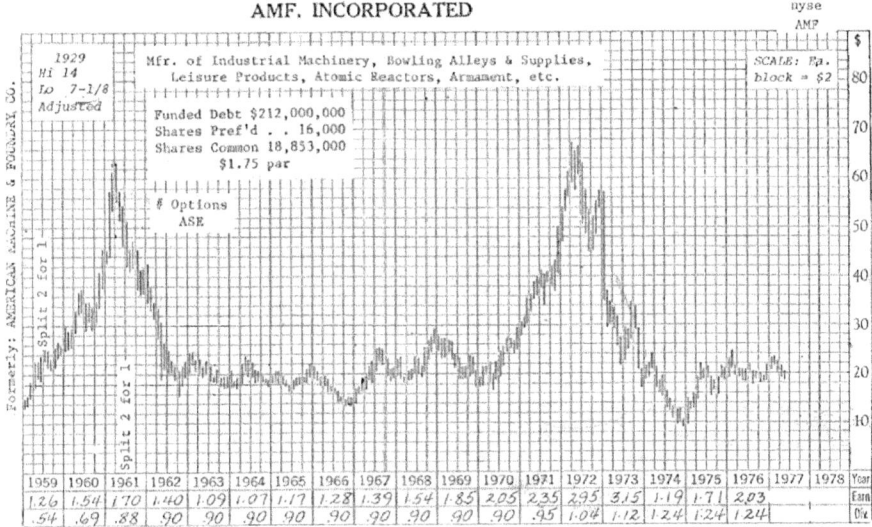

AMF. INCORPORATED

nyse
AMF

Source: Moody's Investors Service, Inc.

Figure 2.1

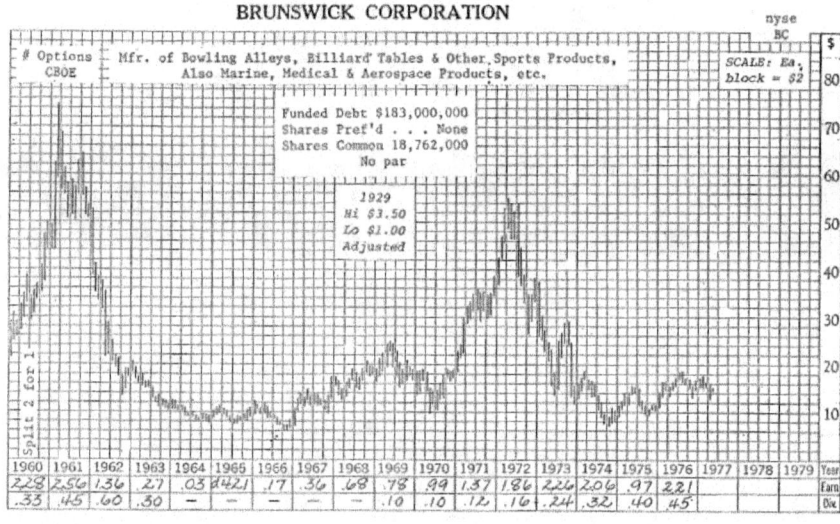

BRUNSWICK CORPORATION

nyse
BC

Options CBOE

Mfr. of Bowling Alleys, Billiard Tables & Other Sports Products,
Also Marine, Medical & Aerospace Products, etc.

SCALE: Ea,
block = $2

Funded Debt $183,000,000
Shares Pref'd . . . None
Shares Common 18,762,000
No par

1929
Hi $3.50
Lo $1.00
Adjusted

Split 2 for 1

	1960	1961	1962	1963	1964	1965	1966	1967	1968	1969	1970	1971	1972	1973	1974	1975	1976	1977	1978	1979	Year
Earn	2.28	2.56	1.36	.27	.03	d42.1	.17	.36	.68	.78	.99	1.37	1.86	2.26	2.06	.97	2.21				Earn
Div	.33	.45	.60	.30	–	–	–	–	–	.10	.10	.12	.16	.24	.32	.40	.45				Div

Source: Moody's Investors Service, Inc.
Figure 2.2

CHAPTER THREE

FIRST HOME RUN

Soon after finding the chart of AMF Corporation I began my search in earnest for the next potential parabolic opportunity. It wasn't long before I came across a chart of Clark Oil and Refining Corporation (see figure 3.1) which showed a price advance from $8 in 1966 to over $65 a share in 1969 and a subsequent decline back to the $6 range in 1974.

Clark Oil operated two refineries in the Midwest and marketed gasoline at prices below those of the major oil companies. Its bright orange and black circular signs attracted cost conscious consumers to their self-service stations located in 13 Midwestern states. Although Clark Oil's earnings record was very erratic, they managed to pay the dividend each year. During the dramatic price advance in 1968 through 1969, earnings only increased from $1.70 to $1.83 per-share, which hardly justified a price-earnings multiple of 35.

I began my buying campaign in March of 1979 with the purchase of 500 shares at 18 1/8. Fortunately the stock traded higher and I was encouraged to buy an additional 500 shares in May at 21 3/4. Clark Oil continued to advance and I bought a final 200 shares at 26 in July. This represented most of my net worth and I was fortunate that my daring was being rewarded. I do not recommend being so overweight in any one stock. But I was young and single then and with hindsight I realize that good luck won out over good judgment. This turned out to be a life-changing event as Clark Oil continued to advance and was acquired by Apex Oil Company in November of 1981 at $74 a share. This again was good fortune because I was spared from the decision of where and when to sell.

I am sometimes reluctant to tell this story for fear that it may sound like bragging, but I think it's important to give a real-life example of how a strategy can play out. The proceeds that I received from Apex oil company for my Clark Oil stock were $88,800, not a bad return for a $25,000 investment made 2 1/2 years earlier. But what happened next was the real excitement. First I bought a brand-new car, the first new car I ever owned, a sporty two-door Delta 88 Oldsmobile for $12,000. That was followed shortly thereafter with the purchase of an engagement and wedding ring for the love of my life to whom I'm still married to this day. The remaining money was invested in 10 stocks that all had patterns similar to AMF and Clark Oil.

Ten years earlier there were a group of stocks known as the "Nifty Fifty". They were one-decision growth stocks that Wall Street ballyhooed as the perfect investment choices. The list started with Avon Products and ended with Xerox. IBM, which was everyone's favorite, was valued at a price earnings ratio of over 40 at its peak in 1973 and by the end of 1974 had fallen to 12 times earnings. The price decline was from $365 a share to $151 and wiped out $20 billion of market value. McDonalds's had an impeccable earnings record and climbed to 80 times earnings in 1972. Although earnings continued to climb the stock dropped from its high of 77 to 21 in 1973 and the PE multiple fell to 21. This group of 50 stocks went from being widely loved to hated and were out-of-favor for the next 10 years as the group went through the laborious task of distribution and re-accumulation. This proved to be a fertile list to invest my new good found fortune.

CLARK OIL & REFINING CORPORATION

LISTED	SYMBOL	INDICATED DIV.	RECENT PRICE	PRICE RANGE (1977-78)	YIELD
NYSE	CKO	$0.60	13	20 - 11	4.6%

MEDIUM GRADE. BECAUSE OF HIGHER COSTS OF CRUDE OIL, PROFIT MARGINS OF THIS REFINER ON BALANCE HAVE BEEN ADVERSELY IMPACTED.

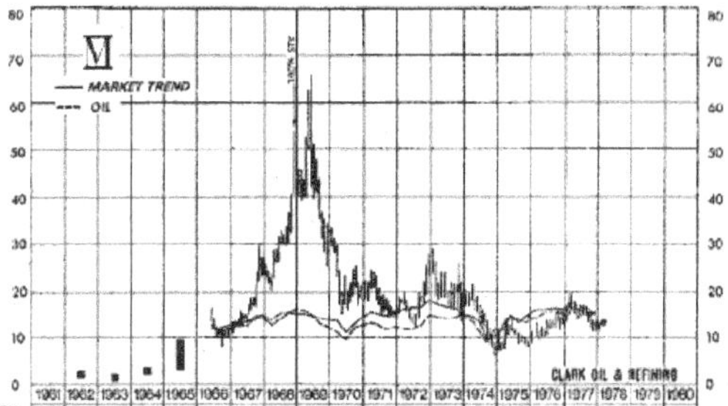

	1961	1962	1963	1964	1965	1966	1967	1968	1969	1970	1971	1972	1973	1974	1975	1976	1977	1978	1979	1980
EARN.	0.07	0.01	0.22	0.31	1.24	1.37	1.63	1.70	1.83	1.50	0.50	1.17	4.29	d	0.74	1.33				
DIV.	STK	—	—	—	0.06	0.34	0.30	0.33	0.40	0.40	0.40	0.40	0.40	0.60	0.50	0.50				

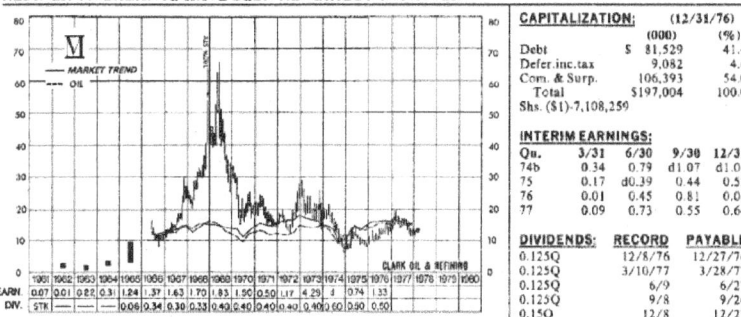

CAPITALIZATION: (12/31/76)

	(000)	(%)
Debt	$ 81,529	41.4
Defer.inc.tax	9,082	4.6
Com. & Surp.	106,393	54.0
Total	$197,004	100.0

Shs. ($1)-7,108,259

INTERIM EARNINGS:

Qu.	3/31	6/30	9/30	12/31
74b	0.34	0.79	d1.07	d1.06
75	0.17	d0.39	0.44	0.52
76	0.01	0.45	0.81	0.06
77	0.09	0.73	0.55	0.64

DIVIDENDS:	RECORD	PAYABLE
0.125Q	12/8/76	12/27/76
0.125Q	3/10/77	3/28/77
0.125Q	6/9	6/27
0.125Q	9/8	9/26
0.15Q	12/8	12/27

BACKGROUND:

Clark Oil is engaged in the marketing of petroleum products on the wholesale-retail level. Purchases of crude oil in the market are necessary, since the Company does not control its own crude oil supply. Clark operates two refineries in Illinois, 11 storage terminals in several states and has interests in several common carrier pipelines. Refined products sold in 1976 rose 7% to 104,289 barrels a day, while refinery throughput rose 8% to 101,095 barrels a day. At the retail level, only gasoline is sold; services such as repairs and sale of tires and accessories are not offered. Company operates over 1,800 service stations. Net production of crude oil and condensate in 1976 totaled 366,000 barrels a 26% reduction from 1975 levels.

RECENT DEVELOPMENTS:

In the fiscal year ended 12/31/77, net income jumped 51% to $14.3 million on a 23% advance in revenues to $887.3 million. In the nine months, earnings did not keep pace with sales. Net income edged up 7% to $9.7 million on a 21% gain in sales to $653.7 million. Company announced that its expansion plans will be reduced for its Woods River refinery in St. Louis. In December, Company raised the quarterly dividend from 12.5c to 15c per share.

PROSPECTS:

The scaled-down plans for refinery will reduce the capital requirements needed to complete present construction. Quarterly profit comparisons should improve from the absence of write-offs associated with the sale of refinery equipment and the completion of maintenance at a Chicago refinery. New oil and natural gas production and higher natural gas prices are expected to make a solid contribution. Other benefits will be a reduction of tanker losses and innovative marketing campaigns.

STATISTICS:

YEAR	GROSS REVS. ($mill.)	OPER. PROFIT MARGIN %	NET INCOME ($000)	WORK CAP. ($mill.)	SENIOR CAPITAL ($mill.)	SHARES (000)	EARN. PER SH.$	DIV. PER SH.$	DIV. PAY %	PRICE RANGE	P/E RATIO	AVG. YIELD %
68	238.4	8.1	12,083	12.2	13.9	7,116	1.70	0.33	19	53½ - 20⅜	21.7	0.9
69	277.5	7.3	13,015	18.1	21.5	7,117	1.83	0.40	22	65¾ - 24⅞	24.8	0.9
70	270.0	5.9	10,671	12.7	44.5	7,118	1.50	0.40	27	33¼ - 15	16.1	1.7
a71	267.0	0.5	3,568	24.7	51.6	7,118	0.50	0.40	80	24⅜ - 14¾	39.3	2.0
72	278.8	0.3	8,342	26.0	47.0	7,108	1.17	0.40	34	28 - 12⅞	17.5	2.0
73	397.1	11.4	30,499	42.0	42.4	7,108	4.29	0.40	9	28⅞ - 13½	4.9	1.9
74	592.8	–	bd7,123	17.5	62.8	7,108	bd1.00	0.60	–	21½ - 6½	–	4.3
75	615.5	1.9	5,237	25.4	89.3	7,108	0.74	0.50	68	14½ - 7⅜	14.8	4.6
76	724.1	3.0	9,439	39.6	81.5	7,108	1.33	0.50	38	15⅜ - 9	9.3	4.0
p77	887.3		14,294				2.01	0.53	26	19⅞ - 11	7.7	3.4

Adjusted for 100% stock dividend 1968. a-Not restated for resale of purchased crude oil. b-Reflects change to LIFO accounting.

INCORPORATED:
July 12, 1934 – Wisconsin

PRINCIPAL OFFICE:
8530 West National Ave.
Milwaukee, Wis. 53227
Tel: (414) 321-5100

ANNUAL MEETING:
First Monday in May

NUMBER OF STOCKHOLDERS:
10,178

TRANSFER AGENT(S):
Marshall & Ilsley Bank
Milwaukee, Wisconsin
Chase Manhattan Bank, N.Y.

REGISTRAR(S):
Marine National Exchange Bank,
Milwaukee, Wisconsin
Citibank, N.Y.

INSTITUTIONAL HOLDINGS:
No. of Institutions: 6
Shares Held: 1,289,169

OFFICERS:
Chairman
O.L. Hill
President
G.W. Jandacek
Secretary
M.R. Durmaster
Treasurer
J.A. Bruss

Source: Moody's Investors Service, Inc.

Figure 3.1

CHAPTER FOUR

COMBINING CURRENT EXAMPLES OF

PARABOLIC MOVES WITH OTHER

TECHNICAL ANALYSIS TOOLS

Schiff Nutrition International and Point & Figure Analysis.

By now, you are probably looking for current examples of parabolic moves. Schiff Nutrition is a great example that has played out in 2012. The attached price chart (figure 4.1) shows the classic price decline from over $20 in 1997 to under $2 a share in 2003. The long base from 2004 thru 2009 is a textbook example of the long period of distribution and accumulation required to set up Schiff Nutrition for a dramatic parabolic move.

A little background about Schiff helps explain the process that unfolded. First, this small company was well run and a serious player in the vitamin business. While Schiff Nutrition was not exactly a household name, several of their products were well known brands. They included MegaRed, Move Free, Airborne and Tiger's Milk nutritional bars. In any event, these were certainly not the kind of media grabbing products to attract stock market attention.

The stock moved steadily higher from under $4 a share in 2009 to over a high of $10 in 2010, which was followed by a series of higher highs and higher lows culminating in a classic move to $34 in late 2012. The final advance was the result of Bayer AG, the German pharmaceutical and chemical company's $1.2 billion dollar offer to acquire Schiff Nutrition. The Wall Street Journal reported the price Bayer was paying as "expensive". However, Schiff's two main shareholders held 85% of the voting rights in the company, and when combined with the fact that once the stock price was over $20, no one had a loss in the stock. To put it another way, the stock was in the strongest of hands. If Bayer wanted to acquire the company, they had to "pay up".

Obviously, we had no inside information that a deal was in the making. However, what attracted us to this stock is the price pattern we have discovered that can lead to a parabolic move. Look at the point and figure chart (figure 4.2); it's a wonderful example of a stock that had completed a long base of distribution and re-accumulation, trading in a narrow range over five years. This was followed by a breakout in 2010 and then the classic stair step advance complete with periods of consolidation preceding each subsequent advance. Finally, an accelerating upward momentum pattern, breaking ever higher before the final move to $34. This point and figure chart was very helpful in keeping an investor in the stock despite all emotional urges to take profits. It should be pointed out that this point and figure chart reflects price adjustment for special cash distributions in 2007, 2009 and 2010. These were substantial, amounting to $1.50, $0.50 and $1.20 respectively. That Schiff could make such real cash distributions should be taken as confirmation that this was a good candidate for a potential parabolic move.

For those who are not familiar with the point and figure method of charting stocks, I would briefly explain that the two most basic types of charts that are used today are the bar or vertical line chart used to display daily, weekly or longer period price activity as well as trading volume. Point & figure charts display price without volume and are more concise, often easier to see patterns build and play out. I like to say, "It's like seeing the same forest from a different perspective". I like to use both types together. I think they complement each other very well. Basically point and figure charts are constructed by placing an X on a chart for each point of advance or for stocks under $10 for each half point of advance and for stocks under $5 entering an X for each quarter point move. I prefer what is called the three box reversal method, which requires a move of three X's to reverse a downtrend or three O's to reverse an uptrend. This may seem complicated; it really isn't. I would encourage you to obtain a copy of *Chart for Profit, Point & Figure Trading* by Earl Blumenthal. Also, Investors Intelligence, publisher of many point and figure chart services is an important resource for charts. Their website is www.chartcraft.com. A great book, *Mastering Market Timing* by Richard Dickson and Tracy Knudsen, has an excellent section regarding point and figure charts. For the more seasoned point and figure fan, Jeremy du Plessis's book, *The Definitive Guide to Point and Figure*, is the most comprehensive guide to the theory and practice of this method. Importantly, it brings home the message that this method predates bar charts and is used throughout the world.

One final note regarding Schiff Nutritional; *Barron's*, a weekly publication I have enjoyed for years, graciously apologized in their November 5, 2012 edition with the following comment: "We found ourselves on the wrong side of a recent call; a bearish item on Schiff Nutrition International (SHF) from Oct. 8. Last Tuesday [Oct. 30], Germany's Bayer said it would acquire the vitamin maker for $34 per share, a 39% premium to the price since our column was published. Ouch." Their word, not mine. Further: "Bayer's deal gives Schiff stock a nosebleed valuation of 36 times consensus analyst estimates of 94 cents in 2012. We still think Schiff's growth is likely to slow within a year, but that's no consolation for us or folks who sold before the offer." I only mention this to point out the conflict between reliance on fundamental information and the importance of technical analysis. Bayer saw value and potential in Schiff's brands with little emphasis on current earnings. The technical analyst saw the strength in the stock price which in the final analysis was what counts.

Just when you think the story is complete, a surprise comes out of the blue. On November 16, 2012 Reckitt Benckiser, the British consumer products company, best known for its French's Classic Yellow Mustard sauce, announced a cash tender offer of $42 per share- $8 above Germany's Bayer offer of $34 per share! Wow! It doesn't get any better than this.

This brings up an opportune time to discuss handling takeover news. Most investors seeing a stock price jump are inclined to rush in and sell in fear the deal will fall thru. I caution restraint at this point. First evaluate the likelihood the deal will be completed. In this case the price rose to almost the $34 takeover price. That's a good sign there is confidence the deal will be completed. Second, management controls the majority of stock so there will be no opposition to the takeover. Of course it's important to check if your position is short term or long term. In a taxable account, you might be only weeks away from the position becoming a long term gain. It usually takes several weeks or months for a takeover to be approved, which in some cases may have beneficial tax consequences for the investor. If the takeover is announced late in the calendar year, you may have the opportunity to delay the gain until the following year.

Not often, but occasionally a counter offer at a higher price may come along, and a bidding war can take place. In the case of Schiff Nutrition, the stock traded as high as $44.50 on speculation that Bayer would counter at a higher price. But Bayer soon capitulated, walking away with a $22 million dollar breakup fee from Schiff if their deal with Bayer was terminated. The deal at $42 was completed with Reckitt Benckiser in December of 2012. The tactics required in a takeover require patience, an evaluation of the outcome and a realization that the first offer may not be the last offer.

Netflix, Inc. Green Mountain Coffee Roasters and GAP Stores

Now that you have seen examples of parabolic moves from decades ago as well as a current example of a small, less well known company you would probably like to see some current examples of larger and more popular stocks. Three companies from very different industries provide dramatic examples of parabolic moves.

Netflix Inc.

Netflix was a very popular movie rental firm where an individual could easily select a DVD movie title to rent at the Netflix website. Depending on what plan subscribed to, for as little as five dollars a month, you could receive several DVDs each month. The DVDs would arrive in the mail in bright red envelopes to be returned by mail at the subscriber's convenience. The turnaround time i.e. from the time the subscriber mailed back a DVD and received the next one could be as little as three days. This was far easier and less expensive than the old rental system which involved going to a store such as Blockbuster. Netflix was the next generation of movie rentals and made Blockbuster obsolete.

Netflix obviously had the world by the tail. They anticipated that movies could be downloaded directly to the subscriber over the Internet and offered that option to their customers. The common stock of Netflix moved from the mid-$20s in 2008 to a high of $304 by July of 2011. The stock then broke down below its 50 day and 200 day moving averages, signaling potential problems. Subsequent rallies in August were weak and the stock deteriorated quickly, plummeting from $200 to $120 in a matter of a week! The company had announced a change in pricing plans which proved to be very unpopular. But this news had come out well after the stock price had rolled over and started down. The use of moving averages is an important way to anticipate the termination of a parabolic move. This is an especially important technical indicator to use once the stock is at such high valuations both in terms of price earnings ratios and in a parabolic rise. A later Special Section will demonstrate the use of three separate moving averages to signal important turns in a stock's price. This will detail the work of a great technical analyst, Dave Landry and his "Bow Tie "approach.

We can see in figure 4.3 a replay in modern times of the same action that took place in AMF over fifty years ago. The laws of supply and demand aren't new or for that matter valuation extremes.

Green Mountain Coffee Roasters

Green Mountain, best known for its famed K-Cup of single serve specialty coffees rode the immensely popular interest in coffee that Starbucks started over thirty years ago. The fascinating chart, figure 4.4, shows Green Mountain breaking out of a six year base in 1999. The advance that followed was truly parabolic ending in 2001. But the decline that followed was very unusual, reversing again upward as this very small company in 1993 began advancing to dramatic new highs before pausing, consolidating its advance as the broad bull market in stocks was ending. But this would prove to be no more than the pause that refreshes as Green Mountain roared to new highs in early 2009 from its October 2008 low. For a stock to show such *relative strength* is of paramount importance. I know not of a more important technical indicator than relative strength. Even if a stock is declining, but the decline relative to other stocks is far less severe, then you have a stock that is inherently strong and will outperform other stocks in an advance. Always buy relative strength. Sell relative weakness.

Green Mountain worked higher during the remainder of 2009 and 2010 before exploding in a parabolic advance ending in 2011. With hindsight, it is easy to see what is a rising consolidation in late 2009-2010 when compared to the 2007-2008 consolidation. This oftentimes marks the halfway point in time and price and that was just the case as that area defined the point between the 2009 thrust and the final parabolic thrust in 2011. They don't get any more dramatic than this. The lesson here is relative strength. If you learn only one pearl of wisdom from this book, appreciate the importance of how issues behave relative to each other.

GAP Inc.

GAP Stores common stock was a market darling during the 1990's, only to become a mature growth stock by the year 2000. This popular priced retailer of jeans and other apparel lost its fashion leadership, and the stock declined much as we saw in AMF. The classic base over the next ten years was a period of distribution and re-accumulation for GAP. During this time, the balance sheet improved, the company repurchased stock and the cash dividend not only paid but increased. The GAP family of stores include Old Navy and Banana Republic which although profitable, displayed little growth. The founding family doggedly worked to close underperforming stores, and open new ones while buying back stock, increasing their ownership in the enterprise.

By 2011 the distribution and re-accumulation phase was complete and the stock began to easily advance to levels not seen in over ten years. See figure 4.5. A stock that could have been bought for under $18 in early 2011 rose steadily, doubling to $37 in the fall of 2012. Of course there's a story. There's always a story. This time, its colored jeans. It's not enough for a girl to have a pair of blue jeans. She now needs a pair in every color, red, black, white, teal, orange etc. Amazing, just like AMF. So the big question is, "does GAP have a parabolic rise?" The individual who bought the base or the breakout has done very well and can now, with the aid of moving averages and watching relative strength, monitor the outcome.

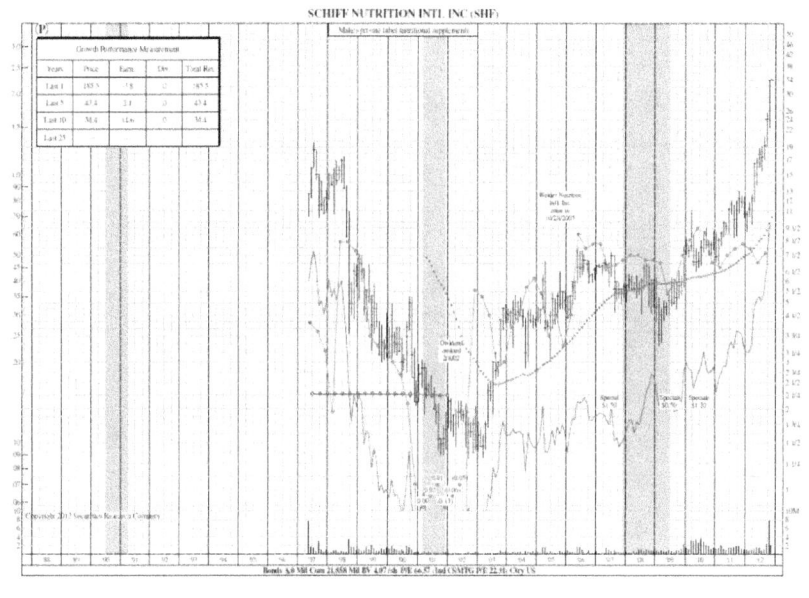

Source: Securities Research Company
Figure 4-1

Schiff Nutrition

© StockCharts.com

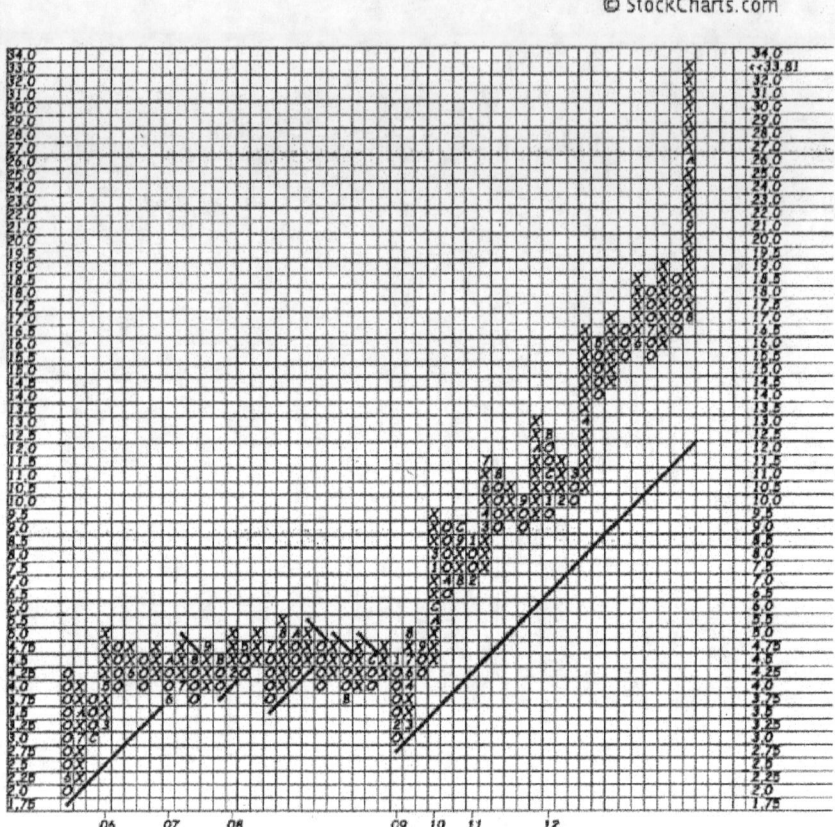

Source: StockCharts.com

Figure 4.2

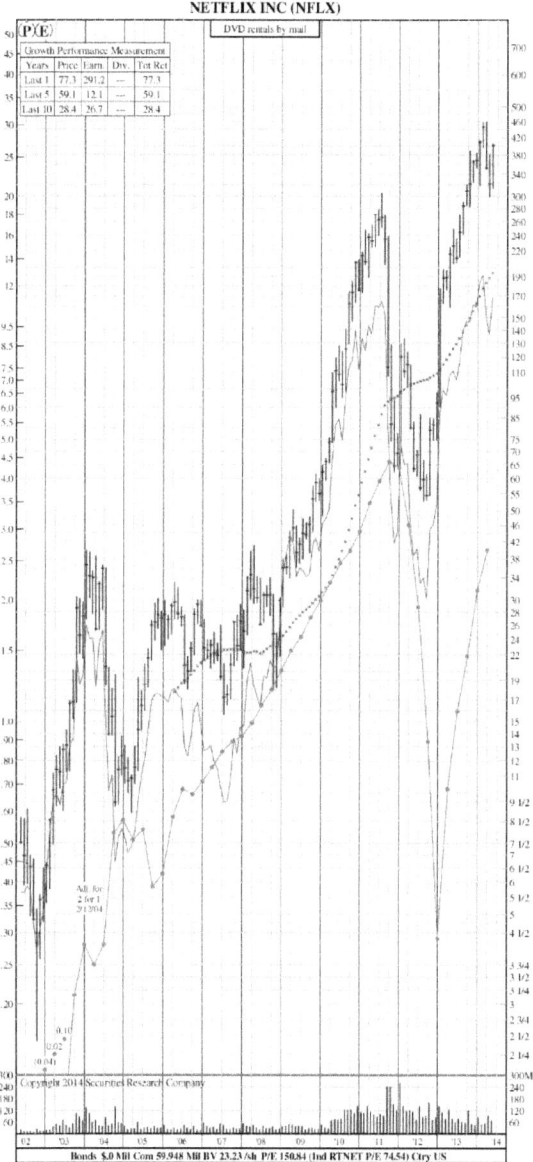

Netflix

Source: Securities Research Company

Figure 4.3

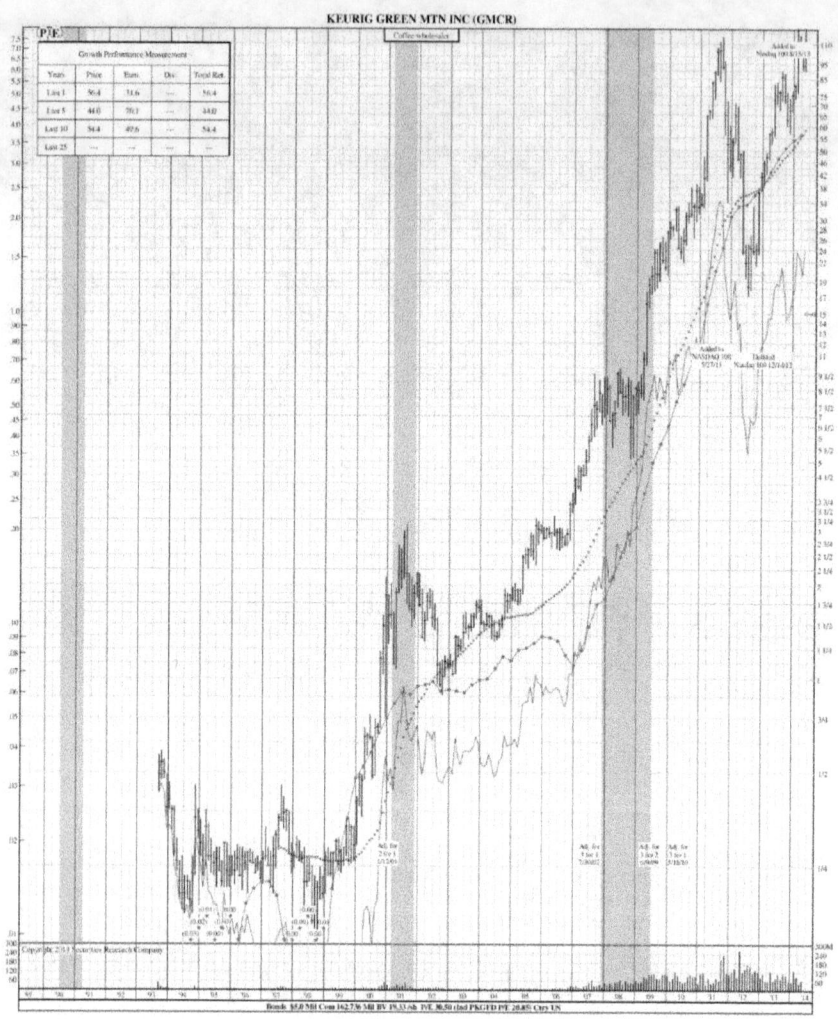

Keurig Green Mountain Inc.

Source: Securities Research Company

Figure 4.4

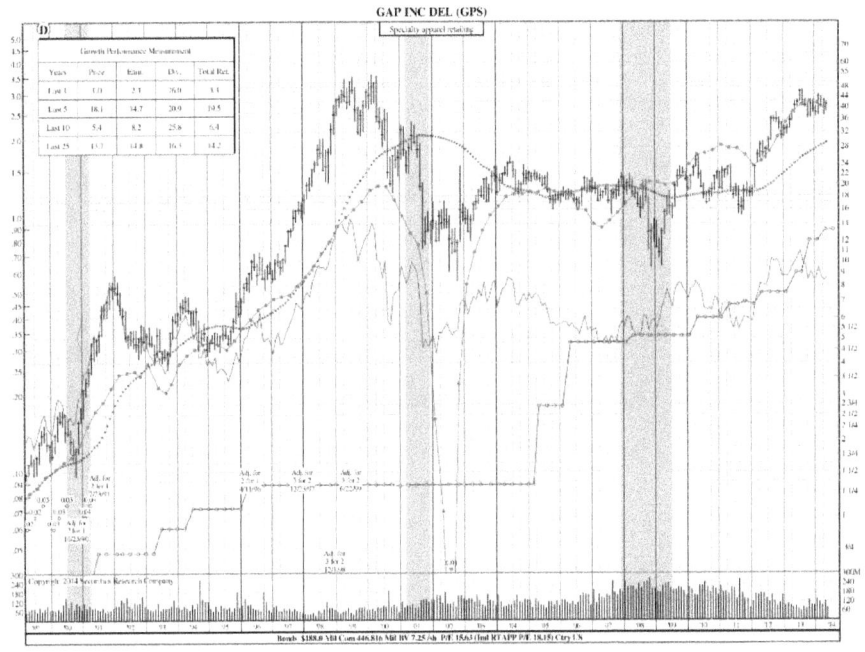

GAP

Source: Securities Research Company

Figure 4.5

PART II

A growth stock has a chart pattern in which

price rises with a positive slope. Where time is

your friend with prices reverting to the mean

over an extended period of years.

CHAPTER FIVE

CONCEPT OF FLOAT

It is understandable, that today many investors are looking for an approach to the market that can be computerized, i.e. a mechanical process that can be programmed to give reliable buy and sell signals. I have tried for years to accomplish this, but have found it all but impossible to write a program about something that is an art, not a science. Years ago, I use to chart by hand the daily action of a stock. I found that doing so required a combination of eye, hand and brain just as a golfer or basketball player uses his eye, hand and brain to determine how to hit the ball or shoot the hoop. Each evening I would by hand enter the high, low and close of the day's price change as well as volume below on the bottom of the chart. I did not realize at the time, but I was training my brain as my eye observed over and over as my hand plotted the activity. Success comes from experience and observing as many real time market moves as possible.

The most basic concept required in analyzing a stock chart is the concept of supply and demand. That's what this book is all about. A stock can only advance when demand is greater than the supply of stock at a given price. Once you fully appreciate this, you will see price movement on a stock chart as the forces of supply and demand playing out. It will start to become obvious, predictable and yes, profitable.

The number of shares of common stock that a corporation has outstanding and available for trading is important to complete one's understanding of the accumulation-distribution process. In order for a stock to advance, demand has to exceed the amount of common stock available for sale at given price. If you think for a moment about having a rare antique, stamp or coin and you know approximately the outstanding number of those items then you can understand how even a small change in demand can push the price higher. Although we don't think of common stocks as being rare we do know how many shares of common stock have been issued. A corporation may have a large amount of stock that is issued and outstanding, but a significant portion may be tightly held and not available to trade. Estimating the float, that is the amount of stock readily available for sale may seem an impossible task but there are several ways to gauge this.

One of the first places to start is with the corporation's proxy statement which is sent out each year to all shareholders and is also readily available at most corporations' websites. See figure 5.1. This is from the Schiff Nutrition International 2011 proxy statement. At the top is a listing of *Ownership of Certain Beneficial Owners* that the Securities and Exchange Commission regulations require under schedule 13 D and 13 G divulging Directors and Executive Officers who have beneficial ownership of a company's common stock. As can be seen these individuals own or control over 8 million shares or 39% of the outstanding class A stock of Schiff Nutrition and can be expected to be long term shareholders. Consequently these shares should not be considered readily available for sale.

The lower section of figure 5.1 shows the *Ownership of Other Principal Stockholders*. The table discloses the number of shares owned by investment advisors and other organizations of Schiff Nutrition's stock. Their total shareholdings represent 3.7 million shares or 17% of the outstanding common stock and can be considered as long term or tightly held stock not readily available for sale. Other examples of tightly held stock would include index funds as well is ETF's and examples shown in the following table.

Float: The number of shares of a corporation that are outstanding and available for trading

Although a corporation may have a large amount of stock that is issued and outstanding, a significant portion may be tightly held and not available to trade.

For example:

1. Officers and directors holdings
2. Mutual fund holdings
3. Index and Exchange Traded funds
4. Trust accounts
5. Cult stocks, e.g. Apple, Starbucks

6. Personality stocks, e.g. Warren Buffet at Berkshire Hathaway
7. Dividend Reinvestment plans
8. 401-k employee stock plans
9. ESOP's (Employee Stock Purchase Plans)
10. Emotional ties

Some of these examples are obvious such as index funds and exchange traded funds. Individuals buy index funds ETF's and mutual funds which in turn accumulate large positions in all variety of stocks. Interestingly, an index fund or ETF is required to invest in the underlying common stocks of the index represented. If it's the Standard & Poor's 500, it has to be composed of the stocks that make up the Standard & Poor's 500 even though some of those companies are not or may not be a desirable investment. But individuals buy index funds and ETF's, which can be industry specific and expect those funds in turn to own those baskets of stocks. Trust accounts are another example where a family organization or foundation has a mandate to hold so many shares of the specific stock for, e.g. the Hershey Foundation owns a very large block of Hershey Company. There are other more mundane reasons for a common stock to have diminished float and these include dividend reinvestment plans and 401(k) employee stock purchase plans.

First & Second Laws of Analysis

Over the past 40 years, first as a stockbroker and later as a Registered Investment Advisor, I enjoyed the luxury of observing how thousands of people managed their investment portfolios. On a day by day basis people seem to be making buy and sell decisions based on hundreds of different reasons. I can see how at one point the theory expressed in the Random Character of Stock Market Prices[1] came to be popular. I observed people buying stocks based on tips, rumors, their children or neighbors place of employment, love of a company's product or even astrology. Rarely did they invest based on quarterly earnings estimates. No matter how serious and well-founded an individual's investment plan might be, I would watch people change course on a whim. They would sell stock for an infinite number of reasons such as divorce, to fund a vacation or buy a timeshare, to acquire a second home, for educational expense or a new car, but rarely if ever because the company missed its earnings estimate. Each day my phone would ring and often, much to my surprise, with the client charging off in a new direction. I came to realize that this was the daily churn that was always there, to be expected and in fact in the aggregate only background noise with small buyers and sellers balancing each other out.

More importantly the stock market was a place for price discovery. By that I mean place where the highest bid and the lowest offer were in agreement. For example if someone is willing to bid $25 for a stock and the lowest offer is 25 1/2 then no trade will take place. If the buyer raises his bid 25 1/4 it might encourage the seller to lower his offer to 25 1/4 and the trade will take place. But if the seller does not lower his price to 25 1/4 and the buyer is determined to acquire the stock he will have to pay 25 1/2. There are other buyers who would buy the stock if they can get it at a much lower price than 25 and there are many sellers who would be willing to sell their stock at a higher price than 25 1/2. The investors that I talked about in the previous paragraph balance each other out. Price movement can better be understood when viewed from the point of accumulation and distribution. If we think of one or more buyers who want to acquire a position in a stock; they may be willing to buy so long as they don't push the price higher in building their position. Depending on the daily trading volume in a given stock, a large buyer might accumulate his position over a number of days or weeks so as not to move the stock. Conversely, a large seller wishing to distribute a large position might also take several days or weeks to unload his position. On the other hand, if the buyer believes he is competing against other buyers he may be more aggressive and be willing to bid higher, paying more to fill his position. A seller fearing a weakening in demand may aggressively accept lower and lower bids in order to dispose of his position.

I don't recall when I began to think solely in terms of accumulation and distribution, but at some point I realized that what I wanted to know; was a stock getting stronger i.e. more demand at a given price than there was supply or was the stock getting weaker because there was more supply than demand. I began to write my own rules. Although these are not rules that had not been discovered by many before me, I decided to put them in writing. The First Law of Analysis states that stock prices advance when demand is greater than supply at a given price and move lower when supply is greater than demand at a given price (elementary). Therefore, an understanding of the float available at a given price and time is key to forecasting price movement. It does seem so elementary to talk about supply and demand moving stock prices. After all in the United States, a capitalist nation, we have an economic system based on supply and demand. The country doesn't need me to explain the obvious. But then why do so many people believe that earnings move stocks? This brings up what I refer to as the Second Law of Analysis that states earnings are *inanimate*. Earnings do not buy and sell stocks, people do (elementary). Earnings may motivate an individual to action or they may not, therefore *the relationship between earnings and stock prices is an indirect relationship*. Many people will argue with this, but at the risk of repeating myself, I am reminded that years ago many people also believed the Earth was flat.

1 The Random Character of Stock Market Prices by Paul Cootner, 1

STOCK OWNERSHIP OF BENEFICIAL OWNERS, DIRECTORS AND MANAGEMENT

The following table sets forth information that has been provided to us regarding the beneficial ownership of our Class A common stock and Class B common stock as of September 12, 2011, the Record Date for (i) each person or entity who is known to us to beneficially own more than 5% of the outstanding shares of our Class A common stock or Class B common stock; (ii) each person who is a director of the Company and each nominee; (iii) each of the executive officers named in the Summary Compensation Table in this proxy statement; and (iv) all current directors and executive officers as a group. The Class B common stock is entitled to 10 votes per share and converts on a one for one basis into shares of the Company's Class A common stock.

Except as noted, the person or entity listed has sole voting and investment power with respect to the shares shown in this table.

	Shares Beneficially Owned(1)				Percent of Total Voting Power
	Number of Shares		Percent		
Name of Beneficial Owner	Class A(2)	Class B	Class A(3)	Class B	
Directors and Named Executive Officers:**					
Eric Weider(4)	7,668,745	7,486,574	35.50%	100%	85.56%
Tarang P. Amin	163,637	—	*	0	*
Ronald L. Corey	102,687	—	*	0	*
Matthew T. Hobart	—	—	0	0	0
Michael Hyatt	36,667	—	*	0	*
Eugene B. Jones	36,667	—	*	0	*
Roger H. Kimmel	172,837	—	*	0	*
George F. Lengvari(5)	59,760	—	*	0	*
Brian P. McDermott	88,288	—	*	0	*
William E. McGlashan, Jr.	—	—	0	0	0
Richard G. Wolford	10,671	—	*	0	*
Joseph W. Baty	171,983	—	*	0	*
Directors and executive officers as a group (15 persons)(4)(5)	8,511,942	7,486,574	39.41%	100%	86.26%
Other Principal Stockholders:					
Weider Health and Fitness(4) 21100 Erwin Street Woodland Hills, CA 91367	7,486,574	7,486,574	34.66%	100%	85.37%
TPG Star SNI, L.P.(6) 301 Commerce St., Suite 3300 Fort Worth, Texas 76102	7,486,574	7,486,574	34.66%	100%	85.37%
GAMCO Investors Inc.(7) One Corporate Center Rye, NY 10580-1422	3,779,795	—	17.50%	0%	3.92%

* Represents less than 1%
** Excludes Bruce J. Wood, who resigned from his positions as the Company's Chief Executive Officer, President and a Director effective March 7, 2011. As of such date, Mr. Wood owned 448,814 Class A shares and held restricted stock units to acquire an aggregate of 417,800 Class A shares. Also excludes Thomas H. Elitharp, who retired from his position as Executive Vice President, Operations and Support Services, effective June 6, 2011. As of such date, Mr. Elitharp owned 69,159 Class A shares.

Source: Schiff Nutritional Proxy Statement

Figure 5.1

STRATEGIC BUYERS, CULT STOCKS,

PERSONALITY STOCKS, AND

MYSTIQUE STOCKS

Strategic Buyers

In the early 1900's, before the creation of the Securities and Exchange Commission, pools operated on Wall Street. These were arrangements where a group of speculators acting in concert would accumulate a *corner*[iii], i.e. a large position in a given stock and in effect diminishing the float and causing the price of that stock to rise. Today such arrangements are illegal, but *strategic buyers,* who are sophisticated, professional investors with large amounts of capital at their disposal, accumulate large positions in a specific stock in anticipation that even the slightest positive news will be the catalyst for that stock to reach its tipping point. That is, the point at which even a small increase in buying can cause the stock to begin to advance. Such was the case in the dramatic rise of AK Steel. See figure 6.1

From a low of just over six dollars a share in 2005 the stock soared to over $73 a share in mid-2008. This dramatic parabolic rise was all the more incredible when viewed over the preceding 10 years. AK Steel Holdings, a New York Stock Exchange listed security, was the result of the merger of Armco Incorporated and Kawasaki Steel in the 1990s. Prior to its rise, the steel industry was out-of-favor in general and quite frankly most of the steel companies were considered dogs. AK Steel traded for under two dollars a share in 2003 before beginning an advance to over 18 in 2005 and then declining to the six dollar range. This should have been the tipoff that this long out-of-favor issue had gone through its lengthy phase of distribution and re-accumulation.

Strategic buyers were accumulating the stock in anticipation of improved times ahead for the steel industry. Sure enough as better times occurred the stock easily advanced over the next three years to the lofty $73 range. The public came in buying as much as they could thinking the good times would go on forever. The strategic buyers who accumulated the stock at lower prices were more than happy to distribute their shares at these lofty levels. The stock collapsed in 2008 to five dollars a share and although somewhat volatile since, AK Steel now faces a prolonged period of distribution and re-accumulation similar to what we saw in AMF. When the strategic buyers sell, closing out their position, it can be quite dramatic. They are not trying to capture top dollar, but rather take their gain quickly and move on to the next deal. They liquidate their position as fast they can, hitting every bid they see.

Cult Stocks, Personality Stocks, and Mystique Stocks

In order to further understand float a few examples of what I call cult, or personality stocks, will help explain how the amount of stock available to trade can diminish for reasons that have nothing to do with the company's earnings. Four very different companies, Apple Computer, Starbucks, Berkshire Hathaway and General Electric fall into these categories. See figures 6.2, 6.3, 6.4 and 6.5.

Apple Computer's founder and leader, the late Steve Jobs, was well known and highly regarded for his technical brilliance and amazing consumer product creations. He inspired his company and customers with the Apple II computer, later the Macintosh computer, then the iPod, iPad and iPhone; all of which brought him world recognition, respect and admiration. Wherever he spoke and whenever he was photographed he was seen in his unvarying company uniform, a black mock turtleneck and jeans. New Balance sneakers replaced conforming wing tips, all of which helped set him apart from other corporate leaders. He had an almost cult following. Apple stock is owned by his admirers and consumers of Apple products. Of course, the success of these products has attracted the attention of other investors, but having a large base of loyal core shareholders contributes to diminished float, i.e. shares available to trade. Being reluctant to split the stock, which as of this writing is over $500 a share, contributes to the mystique while limiting the number of shares outstanding.

This may all seem obvious, but one of the largest common stocks is Exxon Corporation (see figure 6.6) and its leader's name is nowhere as well known. Its stock is bought for an entirely different set of reasons, some of which include a growing dividend and appreciation of a well-run international operation. With over 4 1/2 billion shares of common stock outstanding it is almost impossible for the stock to become scarce let alone have a parabolic move. On the other hand, Apple Computer although smaller with 1.7 billion shares outstanding, has a market cap[iv] greater than Exxon. Certainly the outstanding price performance of Apple stock over the past decade is the result of the stock being tightly held.

Starbucks is another cult or personality stock. Howard Schultz is almost as well-known as Steve Jobs and is the cofounder and head of Starbucks today. This company also is widely loved and respected and deservedly so as they have carefully cultivated an image of a warm loving generous charitable caring company. When you visit a Starbucks store you are greeted by someone with a smile and for many people that may be the only smile they get all day. But that smile from the baristas, the coffee server at their stores, that warm cup of coffee and the knowledge that part of your purchase price is going to help some grower in some faraway land have a better day is all part of the experience. Whenever I see Howard Shultz in an interview with his infectious smile and enthusiasm for his employees and the Starbucks experience I realize this is a carefully cultivated image that is not only good for business but also endears stock ownership and consequently again, diminished float.

The third stock, Berkshire Hathaway is obviously both a cult and personality stock as evidenced by its loyal following and lovable chairman and CEO Warren Buffet. Behind the scenes, Charles T. Munger, Vice-Chairman of Berkshire Hathaway, does the nuts and bolts analysis of where to invest Berkshires money while Warren Buffet is the company spokesman, ever smiling and cheerfully promoting their investment prowess. By not splitting the stock for years, even as it traded at over $30,000 a share, did much to attract attention and glamour to the stock. It became a must-have collector's item in the portfolios of the well-to-do as well as the financial sophisticates. Their annual meetings held in out-of-the-way, off the beaten path Omaha, Nebraska became an event and annual pilgrimage for the devout shareholder. Warren's showmanship was low key but very effective. A carefully honed image of this little old man whose favorite meal is cheeseburger and a cherry Coca-Cola came across in a powerful and favorable way. Most corporations are envious of such followings; where the shareholders always vote their proxies for the management, don't complain and hold their shares for years.

Rounding out the group is General Electric whose articulate, charismatic leader Jack Welch became famous over the 16 years he led the company. Ever smiling, a likable gentleman presiding over General Electric as the stock marched higher year after year. What's more interesting is after he retired, the stock went into a prolonged slump of over 10 years. None of these stocks, because of their size, and the number of shares outstanding have much potential of truly becoming scarce enough to have parabolic moves. But the reason to mention them is to explain that stock can be tightly held which in turn contributes to strong price-performance. One of the advantages I had in viewing thousands of portfolios over the last forty years was to come to understand the motivation that various people have for owning a stock. An individual's personality is reflected in the common stocks he owns. If he or she is a speculator their account probably has high turnover, few dividend stocks and for that matter may be concentrated in one or two issues. At the other extreme, is the opposite of the hot money player, the accumulator of a diversified portfolio of large blue chip stocks. I make no judgment of what's right or wrong but rather I am more interested in who owns what and why. I'm looking for that insight into stocks that are being accumulated, that on balance the float is becoming thinner and thinner i.e. the number of shares available to trade is diminishing.

-----

iii A corner was the result of a pool gaining significant control over the supply of a particular security or commodity so that it was possible to control its price.

iv Market cap is simply the total number of shares outstanding multiplied by the price of the stock. This dollar value represents the total stock market value of the company at any given time. Total shares outstanding should not be confused with float as described herein, which represents the estimate of the number of shares that are not tightly held.

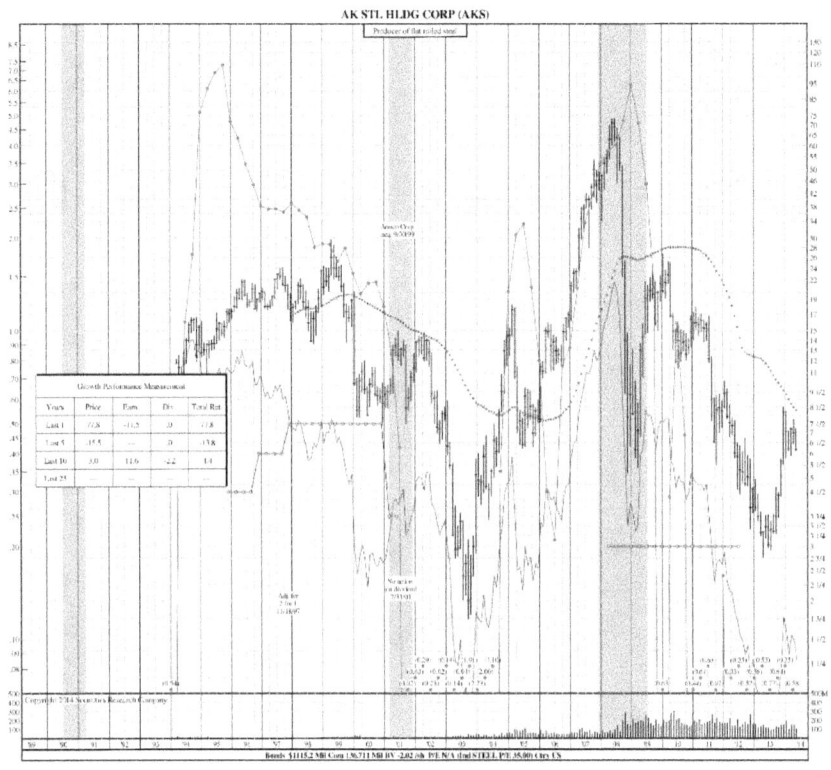

Source: Securities Research Company

Figure 6.1

AK Steel

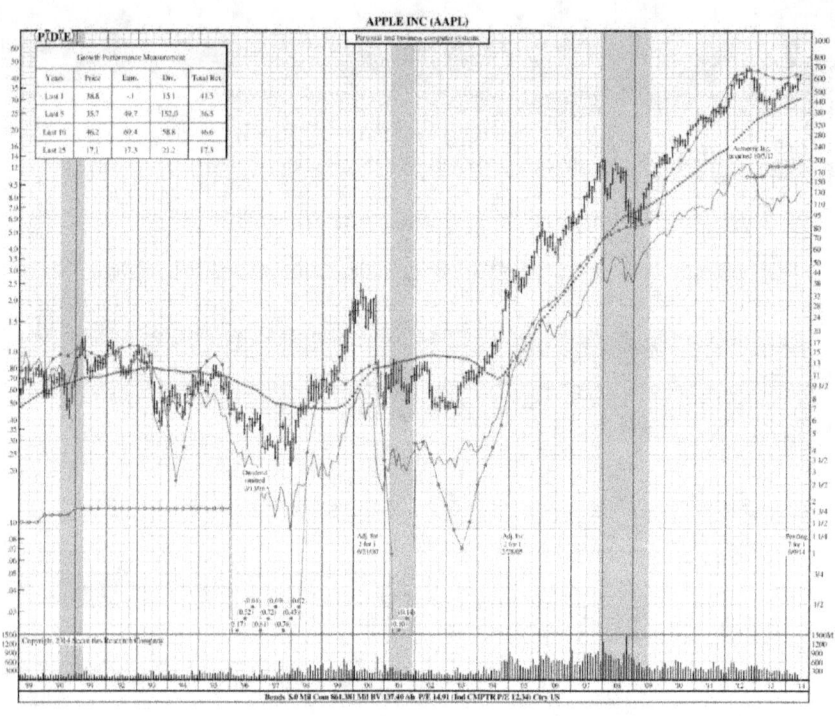

Source: Securities Research Company

Figure 6.2

Apple Inc.

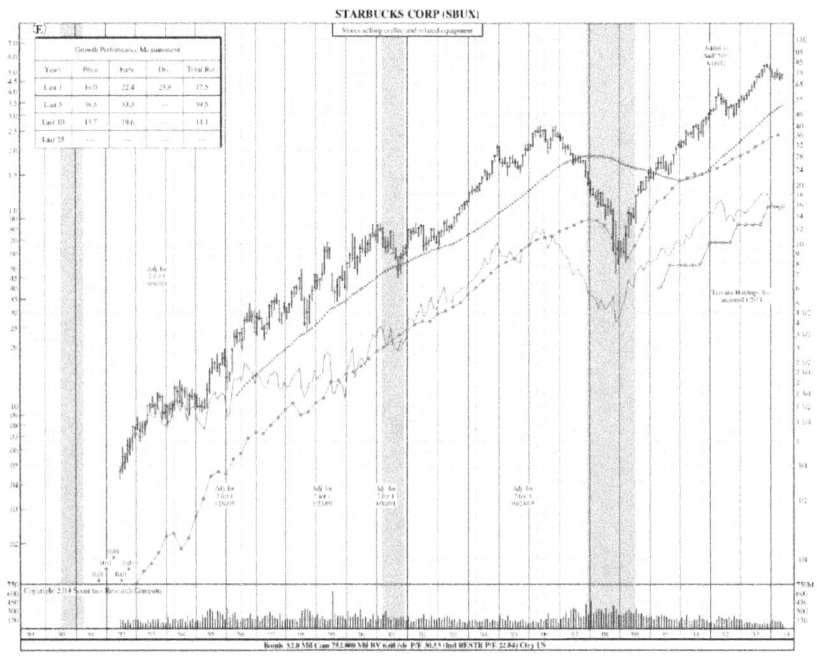

Source: Securities Research Company

Figure 6.3

Starbucks Corp

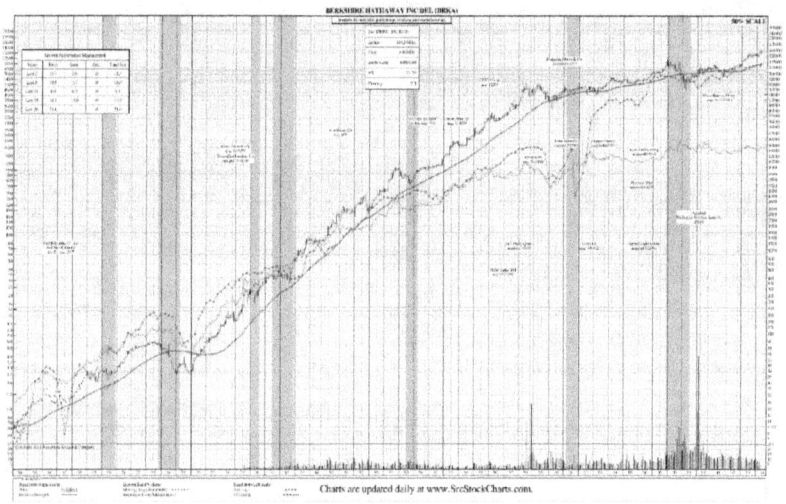

Source: Securities Research Company

Figure 6.4

Berkshire Hathaway Inc.

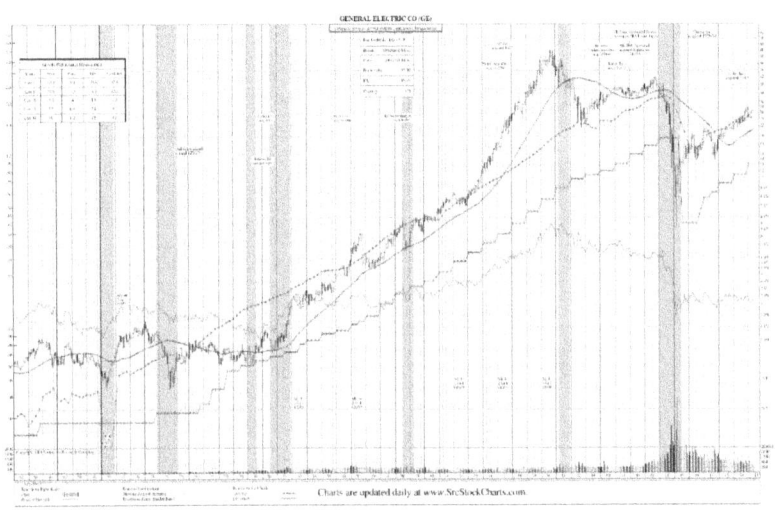

Source: Securities Research Company

Figure 6.5

General Electric Co.

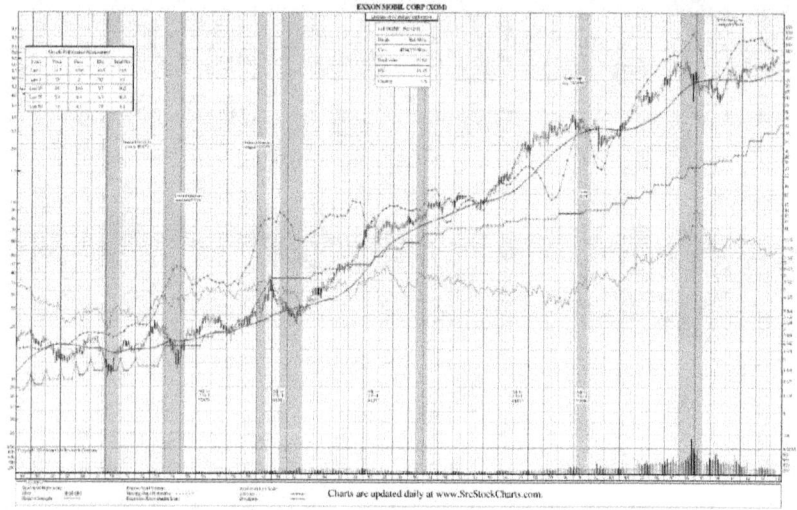

Source: Securities Research Company

Figure 6.6

Exxon Mobil Corp

CHAPTER SEVEN

TAX MOTIVATED TRADES

There is no better example of supply and demand than the imbalances that result from tax loss selling. Individual investors in November and December of each year often review their realized capital gain and loss statement to determine if any tax motivated trades would be worthwhile. If for example an investor has net long-term capital gains he may wish to establish some losses to offset these gains for tax purposes. In the case of short-term capital gains the motivation to offset those gains is even greater because short term gains are taxed at higher ordinary income tax rates as opposed to lower long term capital gain rates.

Not paying tax or at least reducing ones tax burden becomes an overriding factor in the investors mind. The underlying merits of the stock becomes of secondary importance. Any means to reduce taxes overwhelms all judgment. It does not matter that the stock is near the low of the year, sell it. The investor rationalizes that he can buy it back 30 days later and avoids the wash sale rule[v]. What he is overlooking is that he and many other investors are causing an imbalance of supply on the market. What he does not foresee is that come January 1 there will be no sellers of the stock. Few if any ever take a tax loss in January. Consequently there is a shortage of stock for sale after the first of the year. Much to the investors dismay he watches the stock advance during the first few weeks of the New Year. If he had plans to buy the stock back he now is going to pay much more than he sold it for just a few weeks earlier. This advance in the price of the stock is called the *January effect*.

That the calendar can have such a profound effect on an individual's market activity to the point of altering the supply demand relationship for a common stock is a great example of how people influence markets. Over the years I would scan the new low list in November and early December looking for candidates to buy. The peak in tax selling usually occurred during the first two weeks of December and it was possible to buy stocks at incredible bargain prices. Assembling a package of 10 or 20 different stocks, all bought in unemotional quantities, and then waiting until about mid-

January to sell them has proven to be a very profitable way to begin the New Year. Oftentimes a stock bought for four dollars in December could be sold for $5-$6 in January. That may not seem like a big move but percentage-wise it is very nice gain, especially for the short amount of time involved. This may seem contrary to my idea of buying big bases and looking for very large long term moves but it was a logical opportunity that surfaced based on my view of the market from a supply demand relationship. Most mutual funds have a year-end date of mid-October for tax purposes and their tax motivated trades can be observed similarly in the market.

Just the reverse takes place with a stock near its long term high. Few people want to realize a gain in December when postponing the sale to January would throw the gain into the next tax year. This results' in an absence of sellers, i.e. supply in December and a consequently a strong year end advance followed by increase in sellers, i.e. supply in January and a price decline in early January. Accenture Ltd. has been a strong stock over the past 10 years (figure 7.1 see price activity in circle) so you would not expect any year end weakness. A look at Accenture's daily price chart shows strength the last 5 days of the year and weakness the first 5 days of January of the New Year. That's because most stock holders in this issue have gains as seen by the fact it is near its 10 year high. Those wanting to take gains would wait until January to put the gain in the New Year. It's a subtle point, but it happens year after year. The daily chart of IPG Photonics Corporation (figure 7.2 see price activity in circle) shows the stock trading at its lows for the year after a nasty decline from over $70 to under 35 at year end. The stock gapped higher the first day of trading in 2012 and advanced for the next 5 days in the absence of supply having been temporarily exhausted by year end.   The chart of market darling MasterCard (figure 7.3 see price activity in circle) dropped sharply after year end as profit takers waited for the New Year to take their gains. These are three examples showing how stocks near their highs or their lows trade at year end. In the case of Accenture and MasterCard gains are postponed until the New Year while in case if IPG Photonics, selling is accelerated prior to year end. These are the result of short term supply/demand imbalances as compared to our discussion of float where we discussed the long term influences on the supply demand equation.

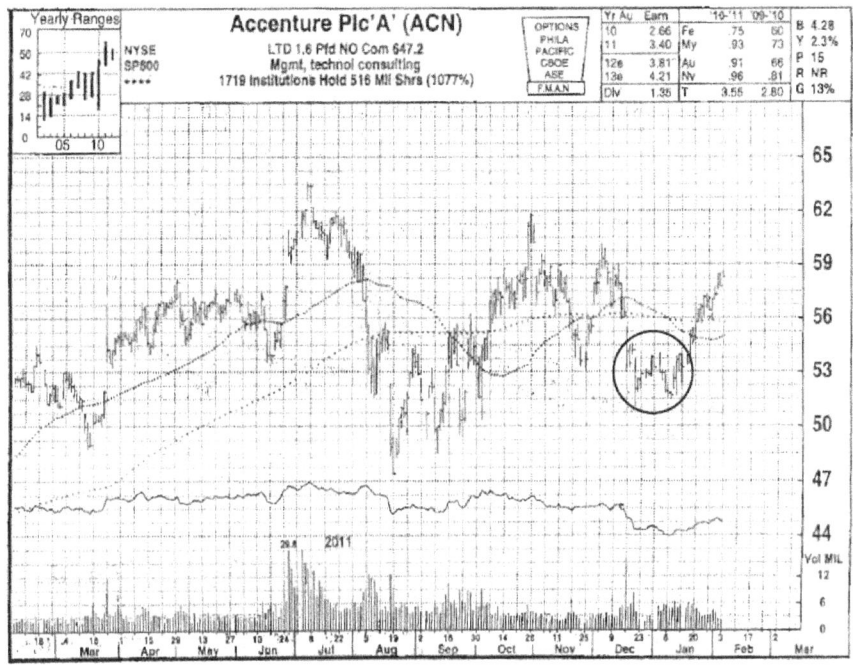

Source: Daily Action Stock Charts
Standard & Poor's Financial Services, LLC
Figure 7.1

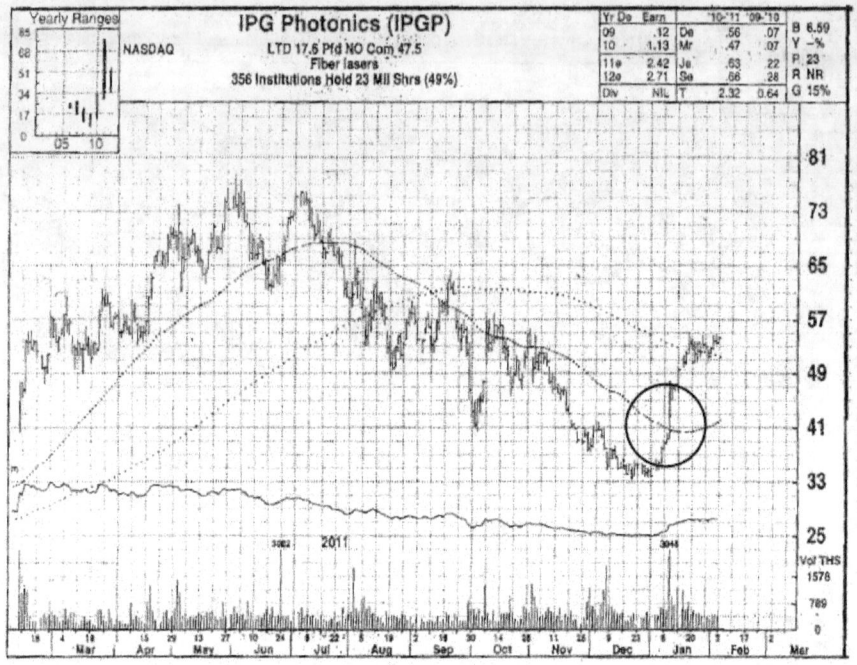

Source: Daily Action Stock Charts
Standard & Poor's Financial Services, LLC
Figure 7.2

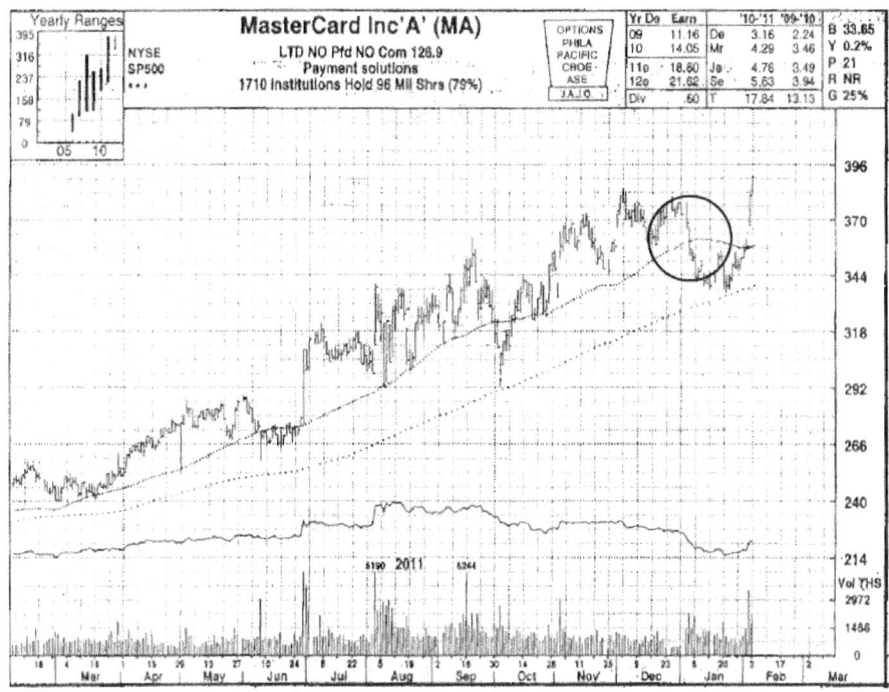

Source: Daily Action Stock Charts
Standard & Poor's Financial Services, LLC
Figure 7.3

---

[v] Wash Sale. An asset bought within 30 days of the sale of the same asset negates the sale i.e. the loss for tax purposes.

PART III

The four general categories where a stock chart

may be classified are; value, growth, parabolic

and cyclical. It is possible for a value stock to

become a growth stock then evolve into a

parabolic stock and finally end as a cyclical

stock.

CHAPTER EIGHT

LONG TERM CHARTS, SUPPORT, AND

RESISTANCE

Long Term Charts

First I should mention the three charting services that I use and a little bit about each one. I have subscribed to the *Trendline Daily Action Stock* Charts published by Standard & Poor's Corporation continuously for the past 40 years. These, as the name obviously implies, are daily bar charts i.e. charts showing each days price action and volume and are published weekly. They show the daily activity over the past year along with 10 and 30 week moving averages of 750 different stocks.   Subscriptions are available on a weekly, bimonthly or monthly basis.

On a daily basis, I go modern and turn to my computer where each evening I review online the daily charts of each stock that I hold or have an interest in possibly buying. For a number of years I have used *WordenTC 2000* service. Oftentimes I will note what action I want to take the following day which allows me to sleep on my thoughts before actually following through the next morning.

Finally, the charts that most help me see the forest for the trees are the long-term monthly charts published by Securities Research Company in Boston Massachusetts. Their *SRC Green Book* of fifty-year charts as well as their 35 year and 12 year chart books are very helpful in finding huge bases as well as identifying those stocks in great growth trends. Companies that have been in existence more than 35 years are shown in the fifty-year book. Younger companies are shown in the 12 year chart book. I usually obtain a set on an annual basis and find the long-term perspective offered by these charts to be of immense value. As a subscriber I am able to go online to their website at www.SrcStockCharts.com where I can view and print up-to-date

copies of most common stocks. I am grateful that The Securities Research
Company has allowed me to reproduce several examples of their charts in
this book.

Before discussing a number of charts in detail I should explain the
layout that SRC uses. Plotted are the monthly price ranges represented by a
solid | showing the lowest and highest point of each month's trading with a
small crossbar indicating the closing price each month. All of the data is
plotted on a uniform semi logarithmic grid and therefore tends to reflect
percentage changes. The price scale is displayed on the right-hand side of
each chart. Dividends are displayed by dashed lines with open circles which
give the month in which payment was paid. Earnings are displayed on a per-
share 12 months ended basis and are shown by a solid black line with black
dots. The moving average shown on the chart by the dotted line represents
the average closing price for the most recent 48 month period. Volume is
displayed along the bottom and represents the number of shares traded each
month with an arithmetic scale on the right side. The gray shaded vertical
strips running from the bottom of the chart to the top represent economic
recession time periods.

The first chart shows the fifty-year history of Brown-Forman
Corporation (figure 8.1), the distillery best known for its flagship Jack
Daniels sour mash whiskey. It should be noted that price ranges are read
from the right-hand scale on each chart. This scale is equal to 15 times their
earnings and dividend scale. Consequently, when the price bars and earnings
line coincide or intersect it shows the price is 15 times earnings. When the
price is above the line the ratio is greater than 15 times earnings and when
below the ratio was less than 15 times earnings. 1972 was an interesting year
for Brown-Forman as the stock price reflected a price-earnings expansion,
that is the stock traded at a higher price-earnings ratio than in the past. This
can be seen by the wide spread between the monthly prices in 1972 and the
black dotted earnings data. 1972 was a year of market complacency
punctuated by the Nifty Fifty Growth stocks. These were companies that
were considered one decision stocks that could be put away and forgotten
forever. Unfortunately they became incredibly overpriced and the almost 2
year great bear market of 1973-1974 not only took the excess out of the
market but brutally punished all stocks. The recession of 1974 was the worst
economic session recession since the Depression and arguably worse than

anything we have seen since including our recent 2008 – 2009 experience. The stock then began a dramatic recovery carrying higher even through the 1982 recession. The decline in 1983 – 1984 was severe as well as the panic in the fall of 1988. It is difficult to ride through such periods even while receiving a growing dividend. After all, these are monthly charts and what may with hindsight appear to be a bump in the road was actually almost 2 years of grief. If one had lightened his position in 1972 it would have been easier to scale back in during the 1974 selling climax. This is one of the reasons why you want to hold stocks in unemotional quantities. In market breaks most stocks decline but only the good quality stocks recover. One is never 100% sure that all of his stocks are without serious problems. But what a chart- the long term holder of Brown-Forman stock has been able to buy a lot of Jack Daniels whiskey!

The next three charts reflect companies that share a common interest in the industrial gas business. These are companies that separate the various components of air into industrial gases such as oxygen, hydrogen and nitrogen which are then sold to dozens of different industries such as the steel, petrochemical, electrical and health care. The chart of Air Products and Chemicals Incorporated (figure 8.2) shows dramatic long-term growth even during a whole litany of crises such as the 1973-74 bear market and Arab Oil Embargo, the 1979 Iranian seizure of US hostages, the prime rate rise to over 21 1/2% in 1980, the Exxon Valdez oil tanker disaster in 1988, and the San Francisco earthquake in 1989. The horrific 9-11terrorist attack in 2001 caused Air Products to suffer a dip in the stock price which with hindsight was an opportunity to buy not to sell. News-wise the past 50 years have been very tumultuous, but then, when were there times that were not tumultuous? Most people act on emotion and sell when news is bad and stocks are low and buy when everything seems the brightest and prices are high.

It's always fun to look at related companies and Airgas Incorporated is just one such stock. Figure 8.3 shows the 25 year price history of Airgas, a company also in the industrial gas business. Although the history is not as long as Air Products, Airgas enjoyed a very dramatic rise from 1990 through 1995 and got way ahead of itself as can be seen by the dramatic PE expansion in late 1996. The ensuing correction lasted four long years before the stock was dramatically undervalued in the year 2000 and then began a long advance for the remainder of the decade.

Praxair Incorporated (figure 8.4) which was the industrial gas division of Union Carbide, then known as the Linde operation, was spun out and became public in 1992. The dramatic rise of Praxair led to an excess valuation in 1997 some six months later than Airgas, as can be seen by its PE expansion and the ensuing correction that followed. The decline ran its course also ending in the year 2000. What's more interesting is the correction that followed ending in October of 2008. The 2008- 2009 bear market ended in March 2009 but Praxair's correction ended the previous October which is a great example of relative strength for this issue. The stock went on to recover to new highs.

Great growth stocks can be found in almost any area, among the most mundane of businesses. A look at W.W. Granger Incorporated (figure 8.5) depicts the dramatic long-term price-performance of this North American distributor of electrical and industrial products. The chart of McDonald's Corp. (figure 8.6) is impressive. Except for the over-evaluation in 1972 and 1999 when the public became enamored with this stock and the inevitable correction to more realistic valuation levels, the stock has been a stellar performer.

From hardware to hamburgers we have seen a wide variety of great growth stocks. O'Reilly Automotive (figure 8.7) the retail chain store selling auto parts has been on fire as well as Ralph Lauren Corp.(figure 8.8) the designer and marketer of premium clothing products. Of course it can be argued the one thing all these companies have in common is growing earnings. But then of course we look at Kansas City Southern (figure 8.9), the railroad that runs north-south through the center of the country and see an earnings picture that over the last decade has been very erratic. A very timely spinoff of Stilwell Financial in July 2000 was indeed a fortuitous event for their shareholders. Prior to this time Stilwell Financial had been a steady income generator for Kansas City Southern and viewed as the more desirable part of the enterprise. Since then Kansas City Southern stock has risen steadily as the growth prospects for this strategically located railroad have become apparent.

Of course no tree grows to the sky and a couple of examples of a maturing or at least once great growth stocks should be reviewed. Johnson & Johnson (figure 8.10) the wonderful healthcare products company had rewarded its shareholders grandly both in stock price and dividends. Since

2002 the stock price has languished, moving sideways in a lackluster formation. Will Johnson & Johnson regain its growth or be broken into several separate companies? I do not know. And then of course there is the great Wal-Mart (figure 8.11) which reinvented the discount department store and was a house on fire from 1974 to 1999. Shareholders here were phenomenally rewarded both in share price and a rising stream of dividends. Over the past decade we have seen dividends continue to grow while the share price has gone nowhere. One thing can be gleaned from all of this and that is, the most dramatic growth occurs once a company develops sufficient size to support sustained growth but not so big as to be limited by its size. The chance of picking one great growth stock is not very good, but putting together a basket of a couple dozen choices will greatly improve the likelihood that you will have a number of real outliers.

One final chart brings home the point that not all long term charts show great growth. The fifty year chart of well-known Goodyear Tire & Rubber Company (figure 8.12) drives home the point that some stocks can meander for fifty years with no net appreciation. This very cyclical company both raised and reduced its dividend numerous times. Although there were several cyclical rallies in the stock, there was never a solid base to create a setup for a parabolic move. This chart does not condemn all cyclical stocks; after all, Clark Oil was a cyclical stock that setup beautifully for its parabolic advance. AK Steel is also another good example of a cyclical stock that had its parabolic move.

Support & Resistance and Other Insights

By now you have probably found this book to be a compilation of technical analysis with an appreciation for valuation and emphasis on wealth creation. There are several general, and what I believe important, insights that I would like to share with you.

I was fortunate to travel to Springfield, Massachusetts in early 1971 and spend the day with John Magee co-author of the book *Technical Analysis of Stock Trends*. He was a kind, wonderful man who took great delight when I showed him my binder of daily hand-drawn stock charts. There were over 100 charts with each stocks daily, high, low and close price carefully drawn with the trading volume along the lower portion. These were done on a semi log graph paper which he sold along with his book. He was quite pleased that someone had read his book and so seriously engaged in charting stocks.

What I did not realize at that time was that by going through the laborious effort each evening, charting stocks by hand, I was in fact training myself to analyze a stock chart. It was an eye, hand, brain activity. Just as a basketball player shoots hoops over and over or a golfer at the driving range hits buckets of balls trying to perfect his game. I doubt that few of you will have a couple of hours each day to chart stocks by hand. I did find it enjoyable and relaxing as I maintained those charts for over 10 years. With the advent of the personal computer and charting software I of course moved on but I miss that daily activity.

But more to the point, I discovered a few insights not covered in most books on technical analysis. Most beginning chartists draw lines all over their charts, showing what they believe are support and resistance levels. They are also quick to identify patterns with names such as head and shoulders, diamonds and flags. I don't make fun of this, I used to do this and I still see patterns as I review charts. But I came to look at stock charts in a slightly different way. First, as a stock advanced it would move to a point of exhaustion whereby the stock would then settle back and rest, consolidate before its next move higher. I became more interested in stocks that were able to make new highs on each advance, understanding that each advance would temporarily exhaust itself and have to fall back before advancing again. If a stock is advancing there is no such thing as resistance. If there were truly resistance it could not advance. Ideally any pullback is to higher point than the previous pullback.

Conversely a stock that is declining has no support or it would not be declining. There is only resistance to rallies. A declining stock at some point becomes temporarily exhausted and there is an anemic rally moving the stock higher but not above the previous high at which point the decline begins again to a newer low. I am amused when I think back to my early days as a young broker, when I wired the research department at the New York home office and inquired about a stock that was not behaving well. We were not allowed to talk to the analyst other than to send a written wire, so I did, asking what they thought of XYZ's chart. They wired back, support at 20. Two days later the stock broke 20 like a hot knife through butter. I again wired New York asking what happened, they wired back "stock broke support". This kind of dribble is what gives technical analysis a bad name. The *expert* in New York didn't know what he was doing. The stock was in its own bear market, declining, making successive lower lows; there was no support or it would've been declining.

Basically stocks are in one of three modes; a stock is either in a bull market, advancing or in bear move, declining or the most common type of activity i.e. non-trending. Declining stock should be avoided. There is nothing to be gained by buying a declining stock which will have to go through a prolonged period of distribution and accumulation before it can advance again. It's highly risky to even try to scalp the anemic rallies. Non-trending stocks are stocks that in general are going through the distribution accumulation phase and if those sideways movements are long enough they can provide candidates for parabolic moves. Advancing stocks of course are where you want to be. All this sounds so simple and so basic it is often overlooked.

A little practical and common sense insight I'd like to share is what I call the *initial syndrome*. What is amazing in the brokerage industry is that everyone or almost everyone is a vice president. There are senior vice presidents, assistant vice presidents, regional vice presidents and just plain vice presidents. I've worked in offices where everybody was a vice president. These titles are generously given out by the firm because the salesman is pumped up by having a title and it conveys to his client some aura of importance. One hidden secret is that it reduces his employer's state unemployment tax which caps the rate the company must pay if the employee is an officer. I've seen people in the financial business that have multiple initials after their name and I am always suspicious because from my experiences, the more initials, the more desperate the person is to appear professional. I know this opinion will offend some, but it is more important to use your own intuition and size someone up rather than rely on initials. One last point, I knew one chap who had taken the test, spent the time to earn the certificate proclaiming his accomplishments; the certificate that hung behind his desk was the biggest certificate I have ever seen, it was 2 1/2 feet high and 3 feet wide and proclaimed that he was *certified*. Of course having a bunch of initials doesn't mean you don't know what are doing but it doesn't necessarily mean you do. Beware.

Late in my career in the brokerage industry I ended up at a luncheon much to my chagrin, next to the president of the firm. I say that because I had to make small talk without appearing to be stupid. This fella had recently been recruited from one of the largest firms in the nation to be president of the brokerage firm where I was employed. In trying to make conversation I asked him; "were there any major differences he found at our firm compared with his previous company?" He replied," I've never seen a sales force sold so cheaply as this one". I was amazed by what he said. He went on to explain that he was surprised by how little was being charged to the vendors of financial products i.e. mutual funds, annuities etc. for access to the firms sales force. It is almost never mentioned, but the sales people or brokers as they are sometimes called must by law act in the best interest of their employer, not the customer. They are expected to recommend, push the company's products. This should come as no surprise. When you go into your favorite grocery store, shelf space is sold by the grocer to those vendors willing to buy the eye level, heavy traffic aisle space. There is a reason there are 50 feet of frozen pizza or Coca Cola is so prominently displayed. Brokerage firms sell shelf space too, but in this case its access to their sales force. It is the independent; fee only Registered Investment Advisor that is required by law to put the client first, ahead of his firm's interest.

Bottoms Up or Top Down

For many, this chapter may be the most important. Introspection, understanding ourselves and how we view investing provides a critical, fascinating and valuable insight that is basic to an individual's success. In a nutshell, are you a bottoms up or a tops down investor?

A top down investor takes a macro view, looking at national and world news, economic trends and more often than not, views and predictions that are published widely. A bottoms up investor tends to take the micro view, i.e. looking at the details of each individual company. This may involve looking at individual chart patterns, relative strength i.e. how one company's price performance compares with another or whatever detailed analysis he or she prefers.

Tops down investors, in general prefer to invest in mutual funds, ETF's, index funds or other investment packages. I am always amused when I'm in a group of people and someone proclaims "I'm a big picture guy." They will then go on to explain that they can't be bothered with a lot of little details. By now you can tell that I am somewhat biased in favor of the bottoms up approach. When you invest in an index e.g. the Dow Jones Industrial Average or the Standard & Poor's 500, you are buying the best and worst stocks in that package. Think how much better your performance would be if you could weed out the unattractive issues. That would require a little work but your time would be well rewarded for the effort.

Too often I hear comments like, "oh I sold everything at the top" or "I got out of the market." When I'm in a group of people and I hear a comment like that, usually there is someone there in the background with a big grin. He and I both know that the fella who sold everything was small potatoes. You will never hear a strategic investor make such a comment. The strategic investor will liquidate his entire position in one stock but usually he or she has multiple positions. The experienced, professional is diversified and in most cases has less than 3% of his assets in anyone stock. Investors who have built large diversified stock portfolios do not act on a whim to change a well thought out strategy that they have put in place. In many instances such action would not only create unnecessary capital gains consequences but would indicate a lack of confidence in their basic strategy.

The bottom up investor does not view the stock market as a voting machine. Unfortunately some poor souls will buy or sell based on news events that have little long-term impact on an individual stock. I have seen people react in the stock market to news of earthquakes, political unrest, riots, and rising hemlines[vi]. They tend to invest when they feel good and times are upbeat. They sell when the markets are down and they are depressed. It took me a long time to accept this behavior. But it has always been this way and always will. The strategic buyer knows this and is grateful that there is someone willing to sell to him at the bottom and buy from him at the top.

MTA Meeting

I remember the first conference of the Market Technicians Association that I attended in May of 1995 as if it were yesterday. It was held at a wonderful old resort hotel in Las Vegas, Nevada. In fact this off the strip hotel was at that time the only non-gaming resort in Las Vegas and is probably the reason why we were able to receive such affordable rates for our conference.

That evening after the opening cocktail buffet we gathered for our first presentation and I was surprised when the speaker, Jack Schwager appeared before our small group dressed casually in blue jeans and a shirt, no tie. I soon came to realize that this small, collegial group of less than 50 technical analysts was more interested in substance then appearance. But even more importantly his presentation made a lasting impression upon me. This author of the book *Market Wizards* went on to explain that his interviews with over a dozen very successful stock traders and investors came to one very poignant conclusion and that is, there is no one single approach to the market that is right for everyone. Further, of all the people he interviewed, no two operated in the same fashion. This greatly encouraged me to continue to follow the path I was on knowing that there was no one right way. Over the years I would come to meet many successful people all of whom operated at least in slightly different ways and some very greatly different approaches. That was what always made our meetings interesting, hearing people compare their various indicators, styles and methods to the market. We each have to find our own way. This book is the culmination of a forty-year journey and I hope it gives you, the reader, a leg up on the road to financial success.

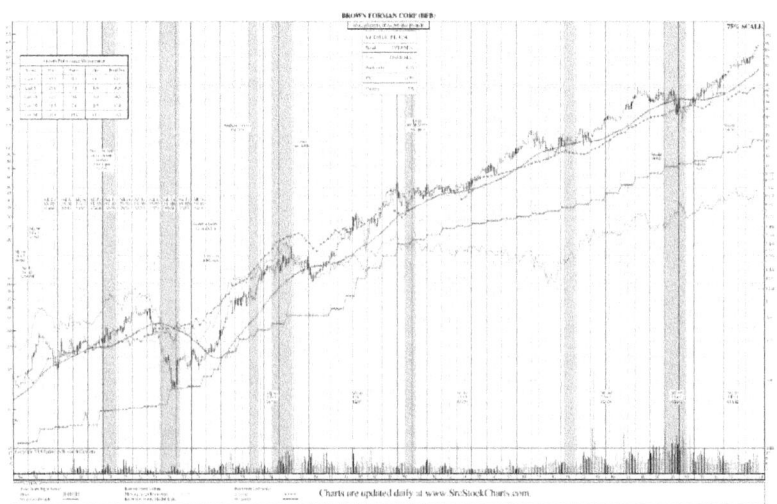

Source: Securities Research Company

Figure 8.1

Brown Forman Corp.

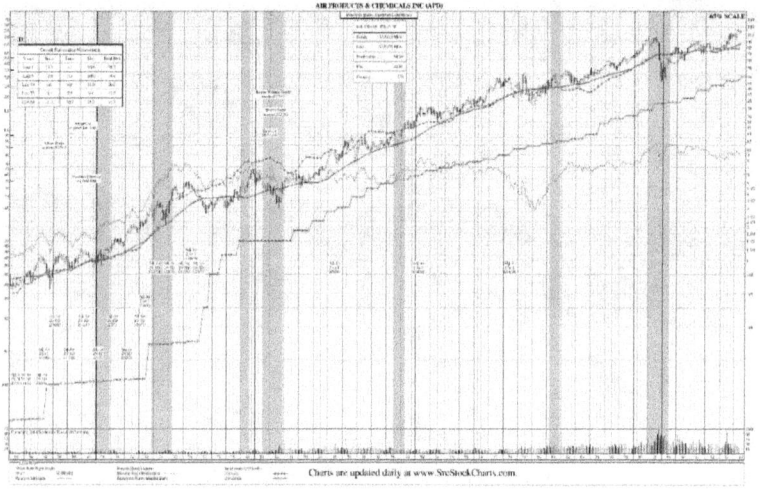

Source: Securities Research Company

Figure 8.2

Air Products & Chemicals Inc.

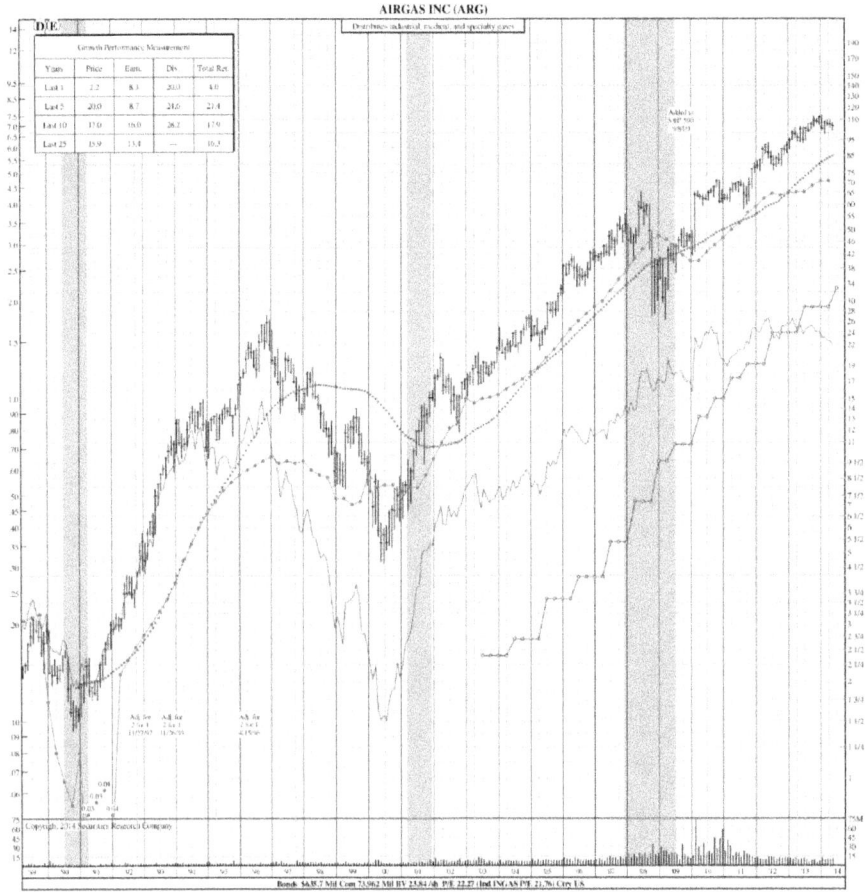

Source: Securities Research Company

Figure 8.3

Airgas Inc.

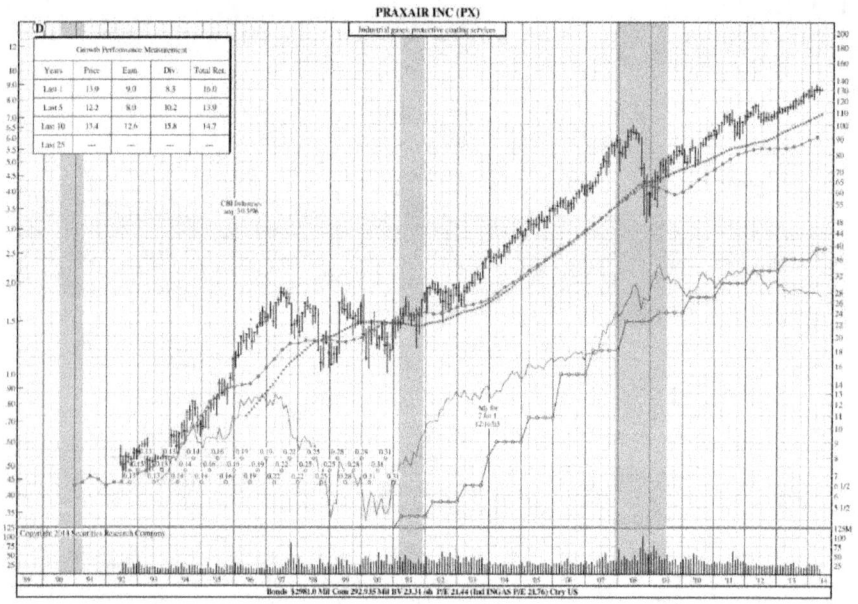

Source: Securities Research Company

Figure 8.4

Praxair Inc.

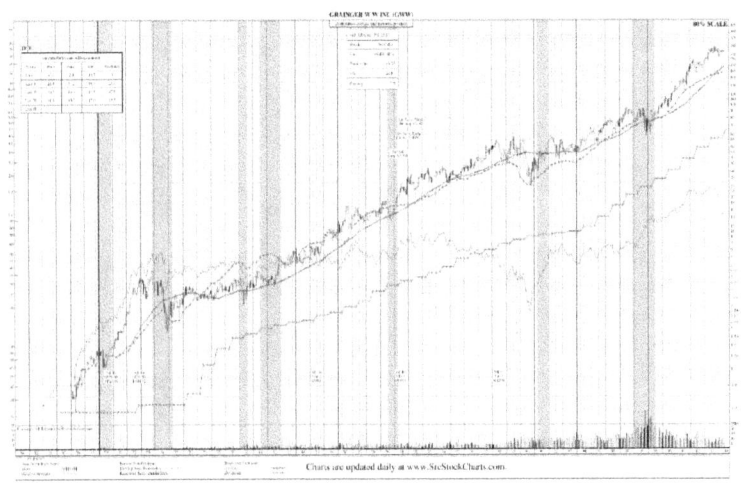

Source: Securities Research Company

Figure 8.5

Granger W W Inc.

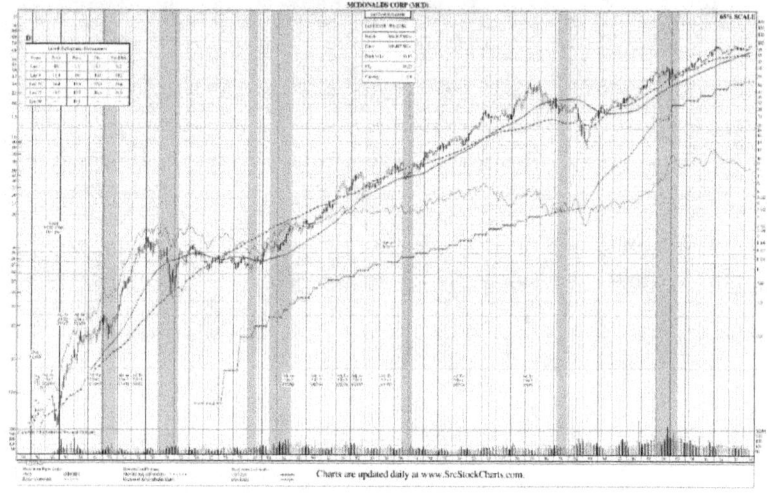

Source: Securities Research Company

Figure 8.6

McDonalds Corp.

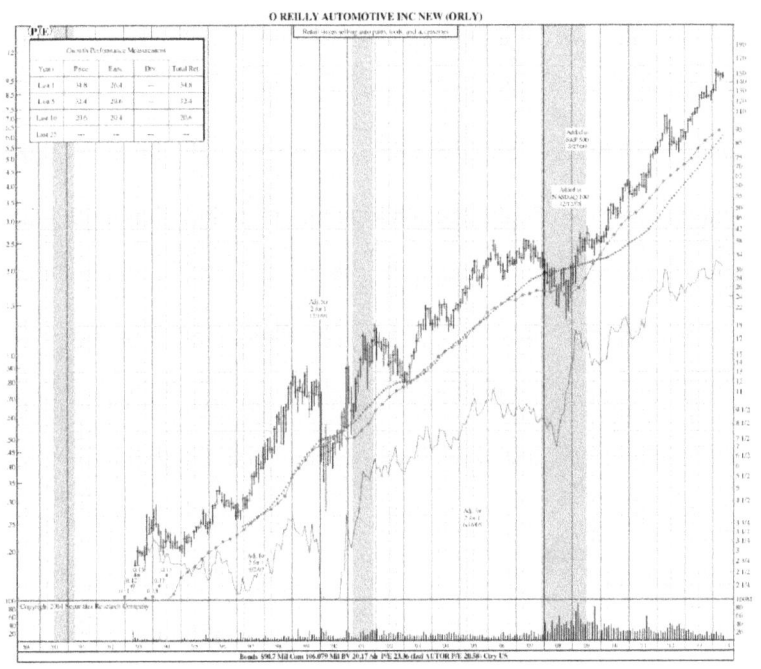

Source: Securities Research Company

Figure 8.7

O'Reilly Automotive Inc.

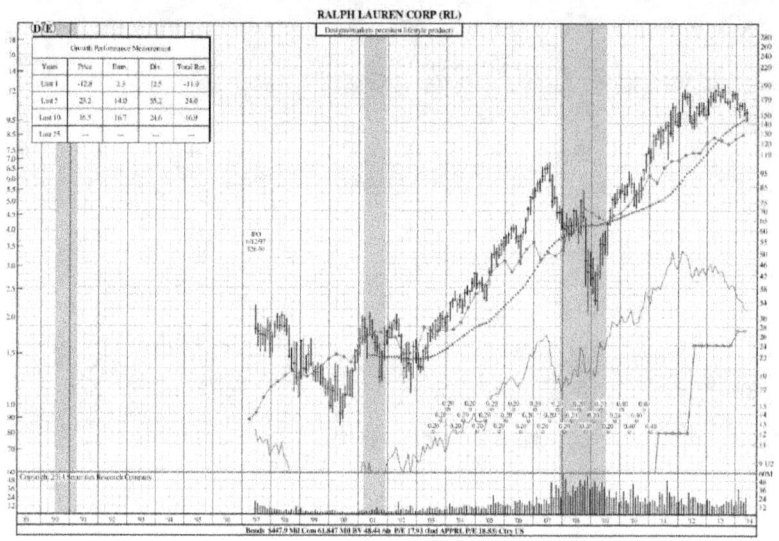

Source: Securities Research Company

Figure 8.8

Ralph Lauren Corp.

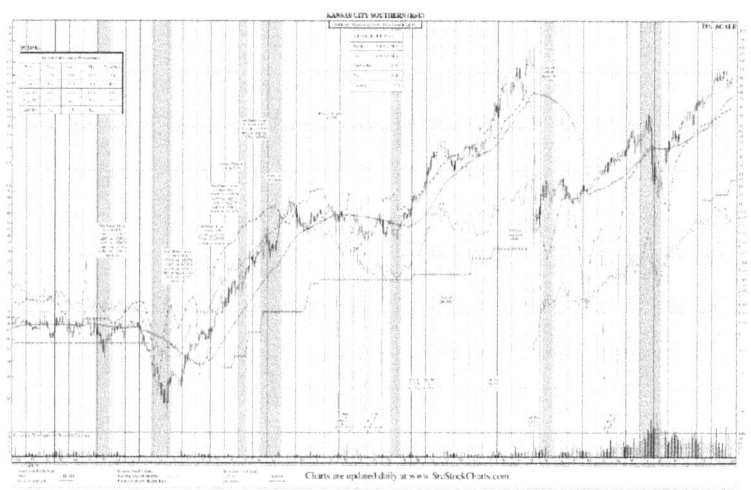

Source: Securities Research Company

Figure 8.9

Kansas City Southern

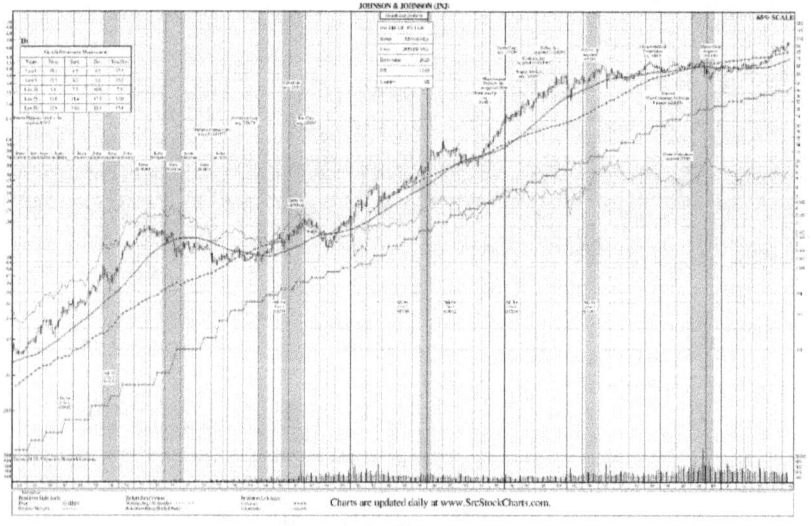

Source: Securities Research Company

Figure 8.10

Johnson & Johnson

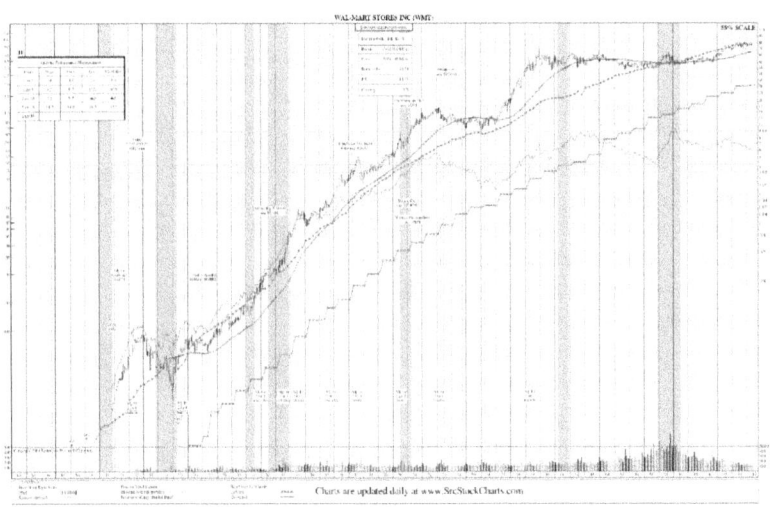

Source: Securities Research Company

Figure 8.11

Wal-Mart Stores Inc.

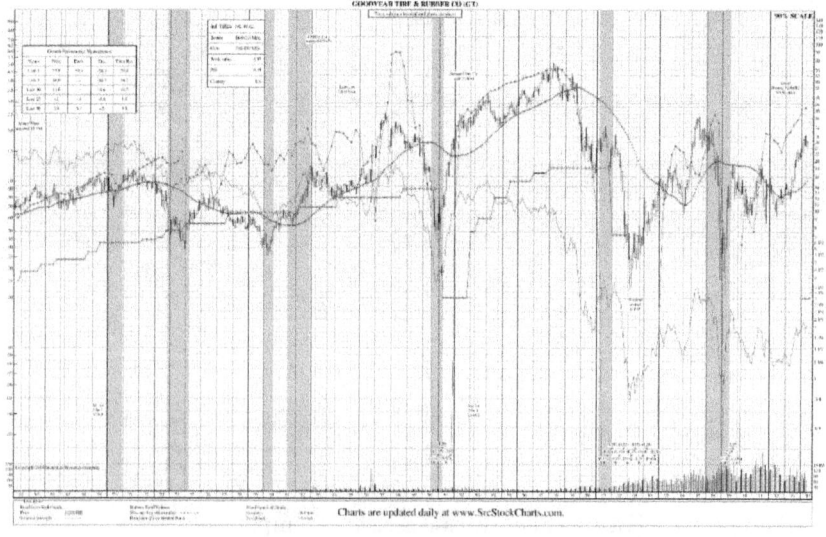

Source: Securities Research Company

Figure 8.12

GoodYear Tire & Rubber Co.

CHAPTER NINE

EINSTEIN AND COMPOUND

INTEREST

"Compound interest is the most powerful force in the universe"
Albert Einstein

Many investors are content to scalp trades for small gains. Although this may be very entertaining, one loss can wipe out several small gains. It also requires a continual generation of new ideas, frequent decision-making, commission expenses and if successful unfavorable short term tax treatment. I find it is much better to look for opportunities that have the potential of at least doubling one's money and in the event the investment does not work out as planned it usually yields at least some smaller positive result.

I often think back to when as a very small child my mother took me to the Ohio Savings and Loan Association to open an account. I had accumulated Christmas and birthday gifts totaling $100 and opened an account that paid 3% per annum. A year later my fortune had grown $103. Trying to be a smart little whippersnapper I heard that the City Loan was paying 3 1/4% and decided to move my money for the bigger return. With hindsight, I don't think the Ohio Savings and Loan was sorry to see me go but probably snickered at thought that the City Loan would now have to suffer what a Dennis the Menace I must've been. I laugh now when I think of what I did to increase my annual earnings by twenty five cents.

Small returns are acceptable when the objective is no risk of principal. But if a person is going to have their money at risk in a stock they should be looking for commensurate returns. I am always fascinated by the rule of 72 which states that when 72 is divided by an annual interest rate the result is the number of years required to double your money. If for example your money grows at 6% a year, then 72 divided by six gives a result of 12 which is the number of years it would take to double your money. If your money grew at 10% a year, then 72 divided by 10 would give the result of 7.2 years. Humorously I think of how many years it would've taken me at 3% to double my money, 72 divided by three is 24 years. But if I buy 10 quality stocks that have large bases, patterns similar to that of AMF, that pay a reasonable dividend, then I can afford to wait the two or three years it may take for hopefully one of those 10 stocks to have a parabolic move. If the remaining nine stocks only breakeven during that period I still have a very nice overall long-term capital gain.

No guarantees, no promises, I'm just attempting to dramatize the power of compounding. If you can grow your money anywhere between 8% and 12% per year, the end result is a wonderful return. Some years are better and some worse, but if you can compound your money at an average annualized rate of 10% a year, it will double every 7.2 years. $100,000 will grow to $200,000 in a little over 7 years, $400,000 in 14.4 years and $800,000 in 21.6 years! It may seem unrealistic to compound at 10%. The attached table and graph (figure 9.1) compares the returns one would achieve over periods of five, ten, fifteen and twenty years at rate of return ranging from 2% to 12%. One hundred thousand growing at 2% becomes $148,595 twenty years later. At 10% it grows to $672,750, that's a difference of over a half million dollars!

One final comment on the Rule of 72, it is a convenient method for mentally estimating an investment's doubling time, but is not exact. An exact calculation gives the result of 7.273 years to double your money at 10% per annum.

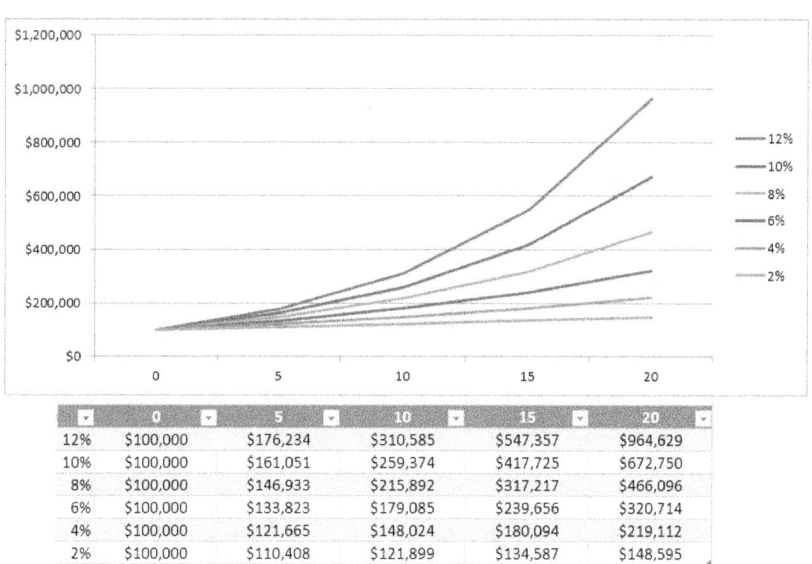

	0	5	10	15	20
12%	$100,000	$176,234	$310,585	$547,357	$964,629
10%	$100,000	$161,051	$259,374	$417,725	$672,750
8%	$100,000	$146,933	$215,892	$317,217	$466,096
6%	$100,000	$133,823	$179,085	$239,656	$320,714
4%	$100,000	$121,665	$148,024	$180,094	$219,112
2%	$100,000	$110,408	$121,899	$134,587	$148,595

Figure 9.1

CHAPTER TEN

APPLE SAYS IT ALL

During the winter of 1966 I invested the small amount of money that I had accumulated in RCA Corp. It's hard to believe now, but back then color TV was the great technological advancement of the day. RCA had completed 24 consecutive quarters of increased earnings and its leader, David Sarnoff was the renowned pioneer of commercial radio and television. Even though television had been invented by Philo Farnsworth prior to the Second World War it wasn't until the early 1950s that black and white televisions became a household fixture. In 1953 RCA's color technology became the standard, but it wasn't until the mid -1960s that sales of color TV became widespread. Since there were few if any broadcast in color there was little reason for anyone to purchase a color TV set. Finally, RCA which owned NBC Broadcasting began to televise shows in color, but it was a long, slow start before color television took off. I can remember my father taking me on New Year's Day to the local radio and television store to see the Rose Bowl Parade broadcast in color. It was an *invitation only* event and we felt privileged to be included. RCA was the market leader, not only in the manufacture of radios and televisions, but vacuum tubes and computers. Obviously, I grew up with a very favorable bias for RCA and was easily influenced by all the hoopla to buy the stock.

Needless to say RCA would not see 25 consecutive quarters of increased earnings. I had made the mistake of buying hype and earnings forecast, a painful lesson. Years later I would read that the famed Graham and Dodd chided Wall Street for its myopic focus on companies' reported earnings per share results and were particularly harsh on the favored "earnings trends." [vii] Graham and Dodd are so often trotted out as proponents of modern-day fundamental analysis. This is untrue. They were value investors believing in analysis to find undervalued securities, not the game of obsessing over quarterly earnings. Wall Street delights in proclaiming breaking news if a company exceeds or fails to exceed its estimate by so little as a penny a share. Nonsense! It is amazing how little has changed over the last hundred years. RCA and David Sarnoff were the giants of the day. Today Apple Computer and Steve Jobs are as much revered and respected as were their predecessors of 50 years ago.

It's even more fun to go further back to the 20s and look at the chart of RCA (figure 10.1) as it made a parabolic rise from under $10 a share in 1926 to over $114 in 1929! It is hard to believe that the price and volume charts today can look just like they did a hundred years ago. The laws of supply and demand do not change. It is often thought that our markets today are more volatile in both directions than in the past. Not true. Nothing has changed. This lesson was so poignantly brought home by a chance event. My office manager was moving to a smaller house, down-sizing, and wanted to unload some old books. She called not to ask if I wanted some of the old books that she had, but as was her personality, to tell me she was bringing them over whether I wanted them or not. I realized I should be kind and accept her books and make her happy. Much to my surprise, she handed me a pristine copy of R.W. Schabacker's book, *Stock Market Theory and Practice* published by B.C. Forbes Publishing Company, copyright 1930, tenth printing, July, 1934. I nearly fell over. "How did you get this?" I asked. She went on to explain that a number of years ago she had gone to work in Philadelphia for a then small discount brokerage firm, Charles Schwab and Company and that her neighbor, an old guy, upon learning of her new employment gave her the book in hopes that she might find it of value. I glanced through the book and was overwhelmed by the almost 900 pages of brilliant insight and information revealed by Richard Schabacker who is the father of technical analysis. This was truly the Old Testament of technical wisdom that I held in my hands. Schabacker's works paved the way for Robert Edwards and John Magee's must read *Technical Analysis of Stock Trends* which was the first book I read on the subject and is still a close at hand reference. It is still available and because of its widespread popularity is considered the Bible of technical analysis.

Good fortune seems to come in waves, because shortly after that I met Donald Mack whose interest in many out-of-print books about the stock market from the 1920s to the 1950s resulted in his re-introduction of some important classic works. One of which was *Technical Analysis and Stock*

Market Profits, A Course in Forecasting, by Richard W. Schabacker, former
Financial Editor of *Forbes Magazine.* This book was first published in 1932 and
re-introduced by Pearson Professional Limited in 1997 through Financial
Times, Prentice Hall. Upon learning that the book was available, I was quick
to purchase a copy. It was later that year, when we went on a short
Thanksgiving holiday that I had a chance to spend some quality time with this
book. I was literally bowled over as I saw price chart after price chart of
parabolic moves that took place in the 1920s. What was especially ominous
was the similarity in those price charts with the current day tech stocks. It
was the fall of 1999 and I realized the tech bubble would break soon just as
the market had in 1929! Most tech stocks were relatively new companies,
unseasoned speculative names with small revenues and little or no profits
selling at astronomical valuations. That was the case with the market in
1929. Our stock market then was immature and so were the tech darlings in
late 1999. I had to act. In early January I put out a press release that our
firm was going to a zero percent weighting in tech stocks i.e. we would not
own any in anticipation of the collapse of this sector in the first quarter of
2000. I lost several clients who didn't hesitate to tell me, "your nuts, tech is
the wave of the future". Well technology is the wave of the future, but it's
also about obsolescence and is very cyclical. In late March the bubble broke
and the rest is history. See Cisco Systems Inc. (fig. 10.2), Microsoft Corp.
(fig. 10.3), and Yahoo! Inc. (fig. 10.4).

Most of the charts in this book are monthly charts, i.e. one bar
represents the highest and lowest price the stock traded at during each
month. Although I do like and use daily price action charts, I find monthly
charts are especially helpful in finding large long term patterns. Parabolic
moves are easier to see on monthly charts. It's important to differentiate
between long term growth stocks, e.g. Wal-Mart between 1995 & 2000
(see figure 8.11) and Apple Incorporated between 2005 and 2012 (see
figure 6.2) and parabolic moves which occur over a much shorter time
frame and usually end climatically as did AK Steel and AMF.

Parabolic moves are the *Royal Flush*, the hand to be dealt, the most
exhilarating stock to own, but when the party's over be glad, as Bernard
Baruch[viii] said when asked the secret of his success, "I sold too soon".

Apple

The chart of Apple Inc. provides the most dramatic present day example of a common stock in an almost parabolic move. As of this writing the stock has advanced from eight dollars a share in 2003 to over $700 a share in September of 2012 for an over 80 fold advance. By any measure this is an unprecedented and historic happening which by rare coincidence brings together a confluence of supply and demand factors in a unique combination never before seen. Apple Computer participated in the tech stock bubble advancing from the $3 level in 1998 to $38 in early 2000 (adjusted for splits) in typical parabolic fashion. The stock then plummeted to its low in 2003. But here the comparison with other parabolic stocks that we have seen begins to change. The pattern of AMF indicates a distribution and re-accumulation pattern that'll usually take place over approximately 10 years. But Apple's distribution and re-accumulation pattern was complete in less than three years. There are several factors that came together in what could be called a perfect storm in a positive sense. Obviously the short answer would be the great product innovation of Apple. But the stock was advancing ahead of the innovations so there must be more here. Apple is a cult stock, a personality stock, and finally a mystique stock.

Value, Growth, Parabolic, and Cyclical

Is there a comparison between Apple and Wal-Mart stock? Sam Walton was the charismatic leader of Wal-Mart who shepherded this company from startup to retailing giant just as Jobs did with Apple. Wal-Mart was a growth stock for many years (figure 8.11) then had a near parabolic rise in the late 1990's which ended not with a dramatic decline but a decade long behavior more in keeping with a mature cyclical company. The law of large numbers dictates that high rates of compound growth is ultimately unsustainable, i.e. if Wal-Mart were to grow at the rate it did in the 1970-2000 period they would become the only retailer in the world in a relatively short amount of time.

In 2002 Apple was viewed by some to be a value stock. Then the stock was trading at $16 pre- split and had almost $8 a share in cash. Hard to believe that Apple could have been considered a value stock. But then it became a great growth stock, rising dramatically (figure 6.2) where it is today viewed as possibly a parabolic stock or at least some variant, a self-sustaining momentum play similar to the tech stocks of over ten years ago. Does Apple become a large cyclical consumer products company? Heresy, that I should hazard such a guess! But, if so, when?

How High Does Apple GO?

It is difficult enough to describe a battle while the event is taking place, let alone forecast the outcome of the war. What I can do, hopefully, is to provoke you to think as rationally as possible about what are the forces playing out in the market. I do not know at what price or on what date Apple will trade at its ultimate valuation. I do believe we have an advantage, some insight into growth stocks and stocks that have parabolic moves; some understanding of the demand forces at work, valuation considerations, and risk reduction concepts that give us a better, not perfect, perspective to act more wisely.

Alone, in the quiet of the night, with as little emotion as possible, look at your chart of Apple, overcome the twin fear that if you sell it may go higher, that if you don't sell it may decline, conquer greed and remember it's just a stock, it doesn't have to be an all or none decision, but rather a personal decision of what you alone in your gut gives you comfort.

[vii] Security Analysis (book), Wikipedia
[viii] Bernard M. Baruch, *The Adventures of a Wall Street Legend,* by James Grant, Simon & Schuster

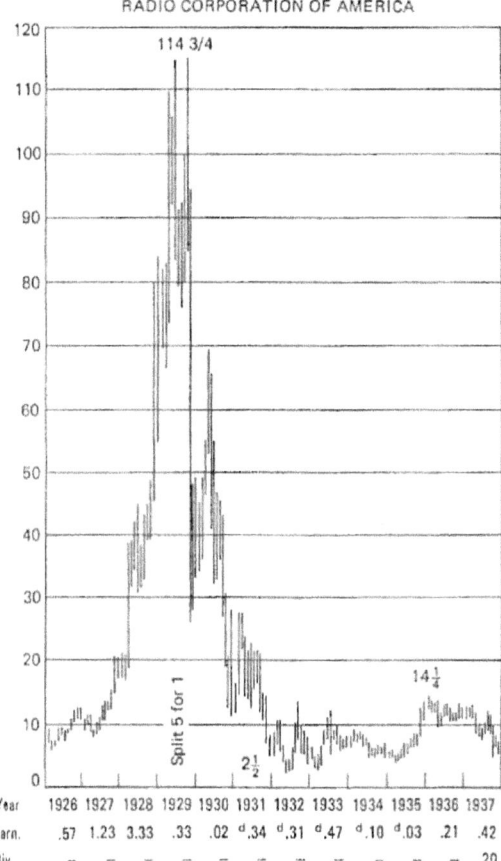

RADIO CORPORATION OF AMERICA

114 3/4

Split 5 for 1

2½

14¼

Year	1926	1927	1928	1929	1930	1931	1932	1933	1934	1935	1936	1937
Earn.	.57	1.23	3.33	.33	.02	d.34	d.31	d.47	d.10	d.03	.21	.42
Div.	--	--	--	--	--	--	--	--	--	--	--	.20

Figure 4.5 Historic RCA smash, 1929–1932 (*Source: M.C. Horsey & Company, Salisbury, MD*)

Source: M.C. Horsey & Company
Figure 10.1

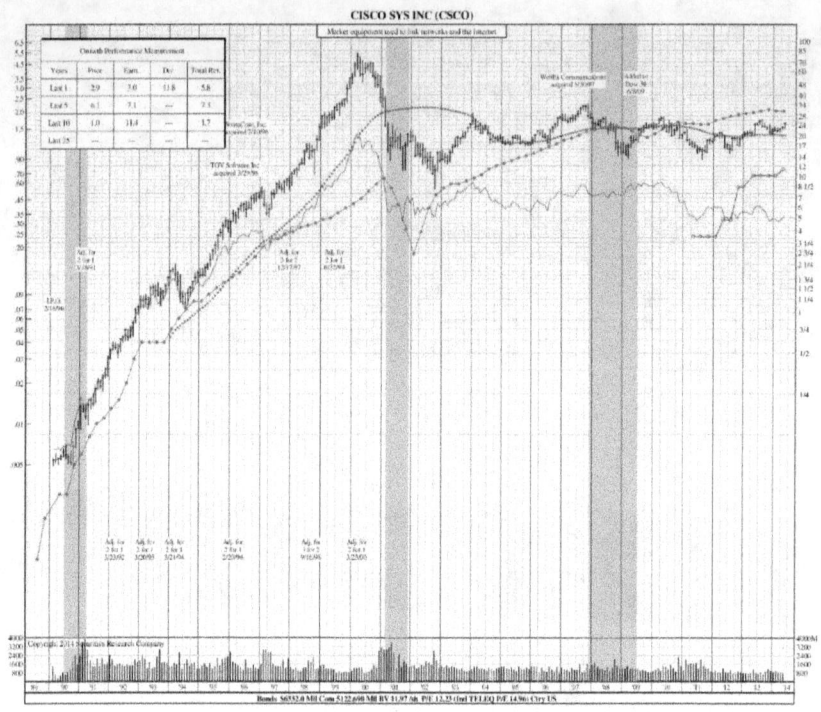

Source: Securities Research Company

Figure 10.2

Cisco Systems Inc.

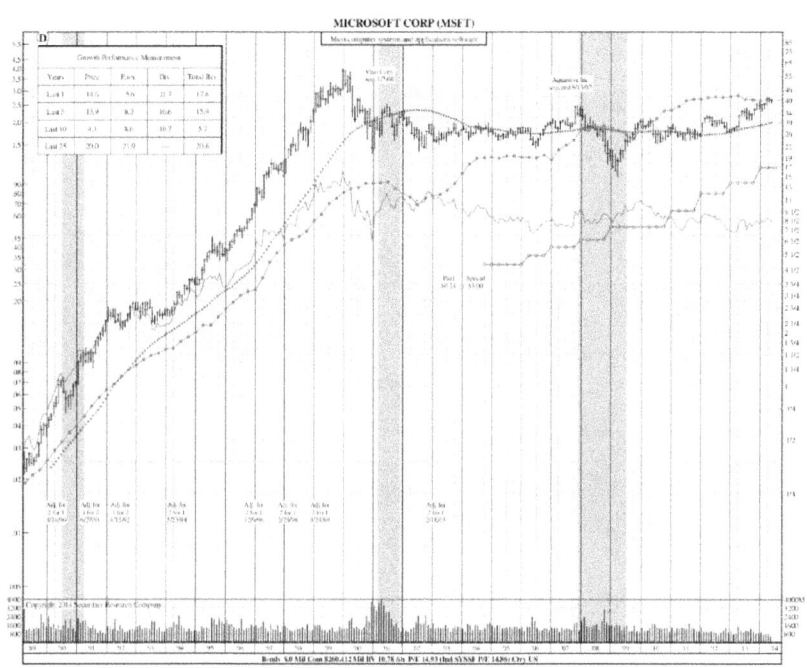

Source: Securities Research Company

Figure 10.3

Microsoft Corp.

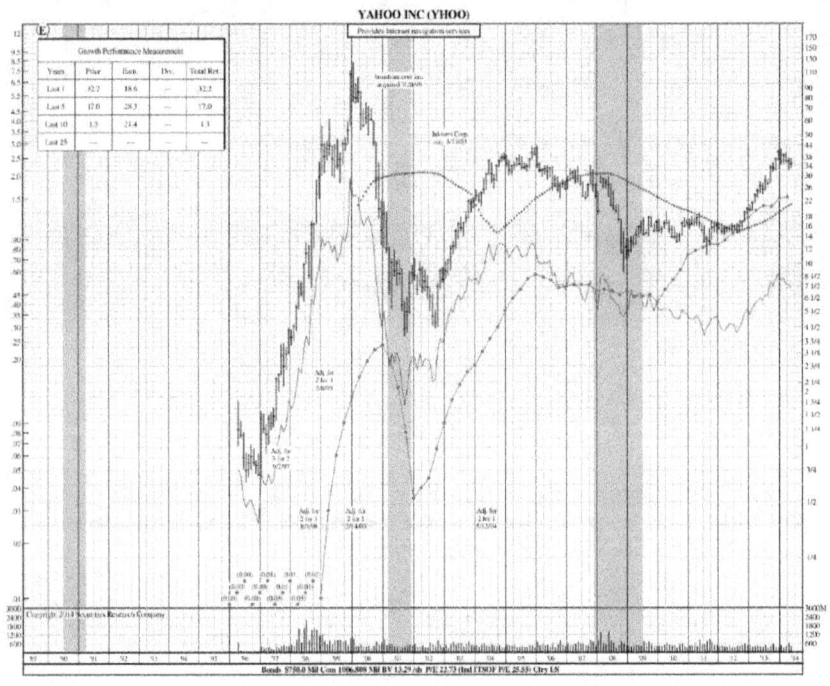

Source: Securities Research Company

Figure 10.4

Yahoo Inc.

PART IV

Vision, Strategy and Tactics. Looking

ahead at what can happen,

researching and then boldly

committing to battle. Success! Victory!

Eureka

CHAPTER ELEVEN

PUTTING IT ALL TOGETHER, A RECIPE

FOR SUCCESS

It's all about thinking big. It's about building wealth, seeing your money multiply ten, twenty, thirty times over a period of time. Thinking big is about real wealth, not a quick small profit and lots of time consuming decisions. Everyone is in a hurry to get rich quick. Good luck. The person who bought Starbucks, Apple Computer, or even Wal-Mart early and held on through thick and thin, not worrying or distracted by the daily harangue truly did get rich.

With hindsight it's easy to see what we should've done. But realistically those fortunate investors who discovered these companies also invested in other situations that didn't fare nearly as well. That's important to think about; because accepting the fact not that every stock you invest in is going to be a winner is an important part of adopting the strategy. The common denominator we look for are companies that are taking a new approach to a product or a service. Starbucks took the simple cup of coffee and offered up a whole new menu and lifestyle. Apple boldly created products that captured the imagination of the consumer. Wal-Mart took retailing that aggressively met consumer demand for low prices. All of these companies were successful in dealing with roadblocks or pitfalls that others succumbed to. Discount retailing is not new; Wal-Mart just got it right. Starbucks saw a market that no one else did while Apple, after years of innovation and struggle, got it right.

Finding the stocks early meant taking a risk and that's why I recommend only a small initial investment. In the case of Starbucks an investment 20 years ago would have resulted in a return in excess of 70

times your money. Such returns more than compensate for those
investments that languish by comparison. All of these companies were
relatively small and as they grew the early shareholders became increasingly
reluctant to sell their stock. As you can see by looking at charts of these
companies it was hard for an investor to ever have a significant loss for an
extended period of time. Success begets success. It becomes a self-
reinforcing lifecycle. The early venture capitalist that put up the seed money
is slow to sell his or her holdings. Early management enjoys seeing the
enterprise grow and thrive not to mention the wealth they are building in
their stock holdings and employee stock options. Customers as well as
suppliers join the bandwagon.

The law of large numbers dictates that every growth cycle reaches
maturity; trees do not grow to the sky. Apple's market valuation now ranks
it as the largest corporation, even greater than that of Exxon. It is
unreasonable to expect it to multiply in size by a factor of 50 again. If that
were to happen, Apple would have a market capitalization of $25,000 a
share, multiplied by its outstanding 1 billion shares or $25,000,000,000.000
(25 trillion). That's not to say the stock can't go higher, but more
importantly to put in perspective the concept of a maturing growth stock.

Looking for the super movers, the grand slams, and the royal flushes
does not have to be a speculative endeavor. It requires a plan, a grand
strategy that starts with thinking big. No brokerage firm is going to find and
recommend a stock to hold for 20 years. They would go broke and therefore
have no incentive to suggest such a thing. So to begin with let's start with an
outline of our strategy.

First we're going to think big. Not look for little gains. Then we're
going to have our eyes open for companies thinking outside the box i.e.
trying new things. Realizing not every new thing or approach will be
successful. Investing only a small amount, less than 3% of our investable
funds in any one idea. Then gauging, evaluating our choices by how they
perform in the market relative to other stocks. This is relative strength and
even if our choice doesn't advance rapidly but at least is showing more
strength than other stocks we should regard that as a sign that were on to
something.

We have talked about two types of big movers, parabolic moves like
we saw in AMF Corporation, AK Steel and Clark Oil and great growth

stocks like McDonalds, Starbucks and Wal-Mart. Each type requires a
different strategy. Parabolic moves are very rapid and occur over a short
period of time, usually one or two years. These stocks must be sold. It is
okay to sell some portion as the stock advances. Do not think you are going
to be able to sell it all at the top. Growth stocks require a different strategy.
It is very easy to fall in love with both types of stocks and the temptations to
brag about your successes are emotions that you need to control. I know it's
hard to do, but when these emotions enter your mind think about the other
companies you bought, that you were so sure you had so thoroughly
analyzed, only later to realize you were wrong.

When I come across a company that impresses me and I believe it
has the possibility of surprising the investment world, I buy it. I may go
months without so much as an idea and that's okay. I don't mind sitting on
cash but when I find an idea, I want to be able to buy and know that it may
be a year or two before I see signs that I'm really onto something. What is
particularly exciting is to have a dozen stocks and two or three that are really
performing well. If there is a dip in the market I may then use that as an
opportunity to add to those positions. If one of those stocks should have a
parabolic move that provides a source of funds to buy four or five additional
positions. Eventually you may have a portfolio of 30 or 40 different stocks a
number of which are growing dramatically. Picture a portfolio that has an
Apple or Starbucks that you can be content to sit with while looking for
additional opportunities. Not all stocks will grow as dramatically as these
but a company that grows at even half that rate is very rewarding and worth
keeping. Diversification is very important and the goal should be to have
several dozen very strong healthy stocks. To wish that you had put all your
money in one of these great performers is a sign of greed. It is much easier
to find the winners when you take fear and greed out of the decision. I find
the best way to do that is to make each investment without emotion, which
is purchased in a quantity that I can sleep with.

In order to find companies that have the potential for parabolic
moves I scan hundreds of long-term charts. One source that I find of
particular value is the SrcStockCharts [ix], long-term charts. They publish a
series of chart books covering periods of ten, twenty-five, thirty-five and
fifty years. Any of these are good starting points to leaf through in your
quest for candidates to analyze. It does not take long, several hours, to go

page by page through the book looking only at the price action that has
transpired over a long period of time. I do not dwell on each or even look at
its name but rather I am looking for long bases and when I find one I then jot
down the name. I may end up with a list of 50 or more companies to further
evaluate. I will then go and look at either weekly or daily price action charts
to better evaluate more recent price action. This exercise results in finding a
number of candidates that are showing more strength than others and this
helps to narrow the number of issues to go forward with. Usually, after I
wind the list down to a dozen issues I may then put these on a daily list of
stock charts to watch over the next few months. During that time I will look
into the fundamentals of each company to better understand and evaluate
the issue for purchase. It is not unusual for me to have ten or more stocks
that I believe can have a parabolic advance. If only one of these advances five
or even better, tenfold, I am then well rewarded. One of the remaining nine
could decline dramatically while the remaining eight mark time and I still
have a very nice total overall return.

There is an old saying that if you only date beautiful girls, you will
only marry a beautiful girl. Not to be a chauvinist I have to add, there is also
an old saying that if a girl only dates rich guys she will only marry a rich guy.
So in the market if you only look for big movers, super stocks, you will only
own the big winners.

When scanning through the chart books looking for big bases I also
come across stocks that are trending higher and this is a good source of leads
for the great growth stocks. Looking back at Wal-Mart and seeing the
behavior in the latter half of the 1970s should have given ample indication
that this was a stock to be looked at seriously. Charts are one great source of
leads but another source comes from observing where people are spending
their time and money. How often do we hear someone say oh I stopped at
Starbucks for a cup of coffee or I've got to go to Wal-Mart to pick up some
item? Paying attention to where people are going, where they are spending
money sounds too simple but it works. I remember years ago when my
office was in the Houston Galleria and I had gone down into the mall to pick
up a sandwich and was amazed to see this line of kids waiting to buy tickets
at the movie theater. I stopped and asked them," What was the great
attraction?" they replied the movie "Star Wars". I didn't think much about it
until the next day when I went out to pick up a sandwich again and there
was a bigger line at the movie theatre. I asked what was so great about the

movie and was told excitedly by the kids what *Star Wars* was all about. It surprised me that they knew so much about a movie they were going to see, but more amazing was the fact that they had seen it two or three times, it was so good. Then when I realized this was during the week and these kids should've been in school- that the attraction of *Star Wars* was that great. I went back to the office and with a little research found that 20th Century Fox Film Corporation (figure 11.1) had produced the film. I looked at the chart and the stock had begun a strong advance and was up that day. Needless to say a parabolic move was under way and I got on board. I don't believe in chasing stocks. Good judgment is necessary to gauge and evaluate your investment. In this case the stock was not overpriced based on its earnings and balance sheet and the move in the stock was coming off a long base. The marketplace was just discovering *Star Wars'* phenomenal popularity. This movie went on to be the biggest grossing movie of all time at that point. Sometimes I go to Starbucks just to count how many customers they serve in a given period of time. You don't have to like Starbucks coffee or for that matter enjoy the movie, *Star Wars*; but if the line is big enough, it just may be one heck of an investment. 20th Century Fox was a parabolic move and Starbucks has been a great growth stock. Both big movers-super stocks.

Pitfalls

There are numerous pitfalls that can be avoided once you grasp the power of an investment portfolio made up of great growth stocks and stocks undergoing parabolic moves. There is a great temptation to go overboard when you find your first candidate to purchase. Often times an investor will take a large position in a stock which will limit his ability to take advantage of other opportunities that will arise later. It's like the golfer who tries to hit the ball too hard and more often than not dubs the whole shot. I strongly discourage the use of margin buying because this reduces your ability to not only ride through a difficult period in the market but drastically reduces the opportunity to add to existing positions or to acquire new positions.

Option trading makes absolutely no sense with this strategy. Buying call options can be quite frustrating when you find time expiring on your call option just prior to the stock advancing. Writing puts will put a little money in your pocket but again if the stock is never put to you then you will have a small amount of money while the stock gets away from you. The option market is for the short term speculator and not for the long-term investor.

It can be helpful if you write down in a log book why you bought each stock. Then when there's negative news about that company or the market in general you can look at the log and remind yourself of your plan and objective. So often an investor gets shaken out of a great position because of temporary extraneous events of little long-term consequence. I have even seen investors sell a stock after it doubled because they are more fearful of losing the gain they have than continuing to participate in a strong advance. Pity the poor investor who sold his Starbucks after the first double. If you are that nervous about your position then sell a small portion, eventually you will gain the confidence to overcome your fear and anxieties and stay on plan.

There is always some end of the world event that at the moment shakes strong stocks out of weak hands. For times like that just take a moment and think, if the world really ended what difference would it make what I owned. When you look back over the last 50 years and think of the wars, recessions, oil spills and all sorts of never before imagined catastrophes then you begin to realize each of those were opportunities to acquire a great growth stocks at very attractive prices. Certainly those were never the time to be sellers.

Dealing with your own emotions is probably the most difficult aspect for the investor. If you start out with $100,000 and are fortunate enough to grow it to $500,000 you will face these concerns again. Then when you reach the unimaginable million dollars you again will question every action. It is one thing to acquire 10 stocks that are not particularly volatile late in their base building process; it is quite another situation when one of those stocks is in a parabolic rise in which the price may advance as much in one day as you paid for it in the beginning. Or to have a growth stock after several splits, move in a day or a week as much as you paid for it to start with.

The most difficult for me and probably the hardest part of a parabolic rise is knowing when to sell. A look at the chart of AK Steel shows a rapid advance to the mid-50 price area and then a quick decline to the mid-30s only to be followed by a rapid rise to the peak at over $70 a share. This middle of the advance shakeout is not uncommon and occurs frequently but not always in a parabolic advance. I know of no way to perfectly time an exit from a parabolic advance. For that matter I can only encourage you to accept the fact that in all probability you will sell some of your stock too soon and some too late and that's okay. For myself I have come to learn that I have a tendency to sell to soon. I like to compare myself to the hunter who is armed with a rifle and two bullets and is being charged by a ferocious tiger; if I shoot both bullets too soon and miss I will be devoured and die, if I wait too long to shoot, the tiger will be upon me and I will die. So I have learned to wait until I am convinced I should sell and them I wait a little longer because I'm always early and then I only sell a small portion. This seems to work for me; it's never an all or none decision. Laddering out as the stock moves higher rewards me with a higher average exit price. Like the tiger analogy, no matter how long I wait my first shot misses, my first sale is too early but that's okay I've got another bullet. Sometimes I'm only selling 10% of my position each time. You probably wonder why I don't use a stop loss order. I have found that a stock can drop so quickly through a stop limit that it fails to execute or in the case of a straight sell stop, the stock may open dramatically lower than my stop with disappointing results. If I have reached the point of considering either a straight sell stop or stop limit, I have found from experience that the best course of action for me is to reduce my exposure by selling some portion and regaining my comfort level. I don't want the tiger to get me.

Does it Always Work?

Does buying stocks with long bases always work? Nope! Understanding that out of a dozen candidates, you will have several small losses, several breakeven and several small gains. But a couple of stocks that double, triple or more will more than make up for the disappointments.

It may be unusual to end a book with a real time example of a disappointment, but then it's only fair to show an example of angst. I bought stock in Compuware Corporation (figure 11.2) in May of 2010 at $8.10 and added to my position in May of 2011 at $9.94 for an average cost of $9.00. The long base covering ten years caught my attention and the common stock of Compuware had sufficient time to complete the distribution-accumulation cycle. The fact that this tech bubble darling had

traded as high as $40 in 2000 and its management appeared to be
determined to regain some of its prior glory encouraged me to take a small
position and add it to my portfolio of potential parabolic stocks. I was even
encouraged by the price action to add to my position in 2011.

But then, as sometimes happens, an offer to acquire all of the shares
of Compuware Corporation at $11 a share by Elliott Management
Corporation, came as quite a surprise and disappointment. Although, this
will result in a small long term gain it is hardly my objective. As of this
writing, Compuware is reviewing the offer and I still hold my shares in
hopes of a better offer at a higher price. A great gain in Schiff Nutrition and
a paltry return from Compuware is a pretty realistic outcome in the hunt for
parabolic moves, but the overall return is more than enough to justify the
effort. Good luck and may you enjoy the challenge as much as I have.

---

ix www.SrcStockCharts.com

TWENTIETH CENTURY-FOX FILM CORP.

LISTED	SYMBOL	INDICATED DIV.	RECENT PRICE	PRICE RANGE (1979)	YIELD
NYSE	TF	$2.40	39	46 - 32	6.2%

LOWER MEDIUM GRADE. A DIVERSIFIED ENTERTAINMENT ORIENTED COMPANY WITH MARKETS AND OPERATIONS THROUGHOUT THE WORLD.

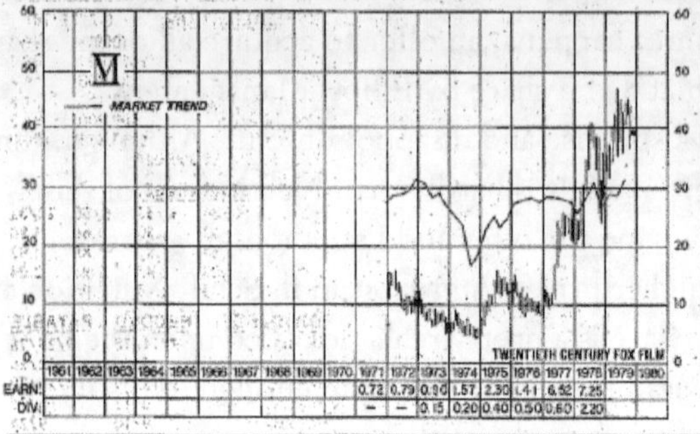

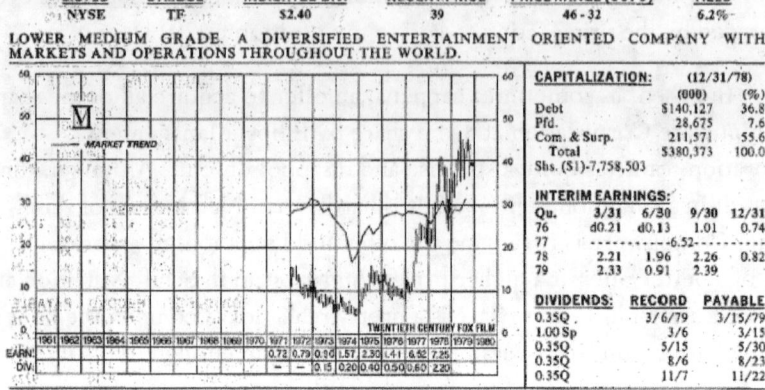

CAPITALIZATION: (12/31/78)

	(000)	(%)
Debt	$140,127	36.8
Pfd.	28,675	7.6
Com. & Surp.	211,571	55.6
Total	$380,373	100.0

Shs. ($1)-7,758,503

INTERIM EARNINGS:

Qu.	3/31	6/30	9/30	12/31
76	d0.21	d0.13	1.01	0.74
77	-----------6.52-----------			
78	2.21	1.96	2.26	0.82
79	2.33	0.91	2.39	

DIVIDENDS:

	RECORD	PAYABLE
0.35Q	3/6/79	3/15/79
1.00 Sp	3/6	3/15
0.35Q	5/15	5/30
0.35Q	8/6	8/23
0.35Q	11/7	11/22

BACKGROUND:

Twentieth Century-Fox Film Corp. is engaged in motion picture production and distribution, television program production and distribution, international theatres, television broadcasting, film processing, phonograph records, music publishing, soft drink bottling and skiing operations. The Company operates about 138 theatres outside the U.S. and owns and operates KMSP-TV, Minneapolis, Min.; KTVX-TV, Salt Lake City, Ut.; and KMOL-TV, San Antonio, Tx. Revenues (and income) at 12//31/78 were as follows: film entertainment, 66.8% (85.1%); international theatre, 8.5% (7.1%); film processing, 3.4% (-0.1%); television stations, 5.2% (12.9%); record and music publishing, 2.3% (-10.2%); soft drink bottling, 13% (6.4%).

RECENT DEVELOPMENTS:

For the quarter ending 9/29/79, net income moved up 7% to $19.7 million. Revenues increased 18% to $189.6 million. In the twelve months, net income declined 10% to $46.5 million on revenues of $496.3 million, up 6%. Benefiting net income was a $40,000 loss in the Record and Music division as compared with a $3.8 million loss last year, $1.6 million in income from the acquisiton of Pebble Beach Corp., a 5.1% gain in Television Broadcasting income and a $.7 million in income from Film Processing.

PROSPECTS:

The Company's profitability should improve in the near future with the booking in 1979 of several major feature film licensing contracts with the CBS and NBC Networks. The record and music publishing operations should benefit from the agreement with RCA Corp. to market all the Company's record products. Over the long term, earnings should continue to show substantial growth as the Company, through acquisitions, becomes more diversified.

STATISTICS:

YEAR	GROSS REVS. ($mill.)	OPER. PROFIT MARGIN %	NET INCOME ($000)	WORK CAP. ($mill.)	SENIOR CAPITAL ($mill.)	SHARES (000)	EARN. PER SH.$	DIV. PER SH.$	DIV. PAY. %	PRICE RANGE	P/E RATIO	AVG. YIELD %
72	201.4	8.5	a6,800	59.7	55.5	8,562	a0.79	Nil	–	17 - 8⅝	16.2	–
73	253.5	7.9	a7,700	34.4	63.9	8,521	a0.90	0.15	17	12⅜ - 5	9.7	1.7
74	281.9	9.4	ab12,400	21.4	63.9	7,532	ab1.57	0.20	13	13 - 9⅛	7.1	1.8
75	342.7	10.6	a17,400	32.8	82.6	7,548	a2.30	0.40	17	15½ - 15⅛	4.5	3.9
76	355.0	7.1	10,700	34.2	94.7	7,570	1.41	0.50	36	15 - 8⅜	8.3	4.3
77	506.8	16.6	50,800	76.6	98.1	7,697	6.52	0.60	9	26⅝ - 9⅞	2.8	3.3
78	610.9	15.6	58,390	114.7	168.8	7,759	7.25	2.20	30	40¾ - 20⅝	4.2	7.2

a-Before extraord. items. b-Before loss discont. oper.

INCORPORATED:
July 22, 1952 – Delaware

PRINCIPAL OFFICE:
10201 West Pico Blvd.
Los Angeles, CA 90035
Tel: (213) 277-2211

ANNUAL MEETING:
Fifth Thursday in April

NUMBER OF STOCKHOLDERS:
16,500

TRANSFER AGENT(S):
First National Bank of Boston, Boston, Mass.

REGISTRAR(S):
First National Bank of Bsoton, Boston, Mass.

INSTITUTIONAL HOLDINGS:
No. of Institutions: 58
Shares Held: 2,974,358

OFFICERS:
Chmn. & Ch. Exec.Off., D.C. Stanfill; Vice-Chmn. & C.O.O., A.J. Herschfield; President, C.J. LaBonte; Vice Pres.-Fin. & Adm., E.A. Bowen; Vice-Pres & Sec., J.C. Gallagher; Vice-Pres. & Treas., E.L. Marshall

Source: Moody's Investors Service, Inc.

Figure 11.1

COMPUWARE CORP (CPWR)

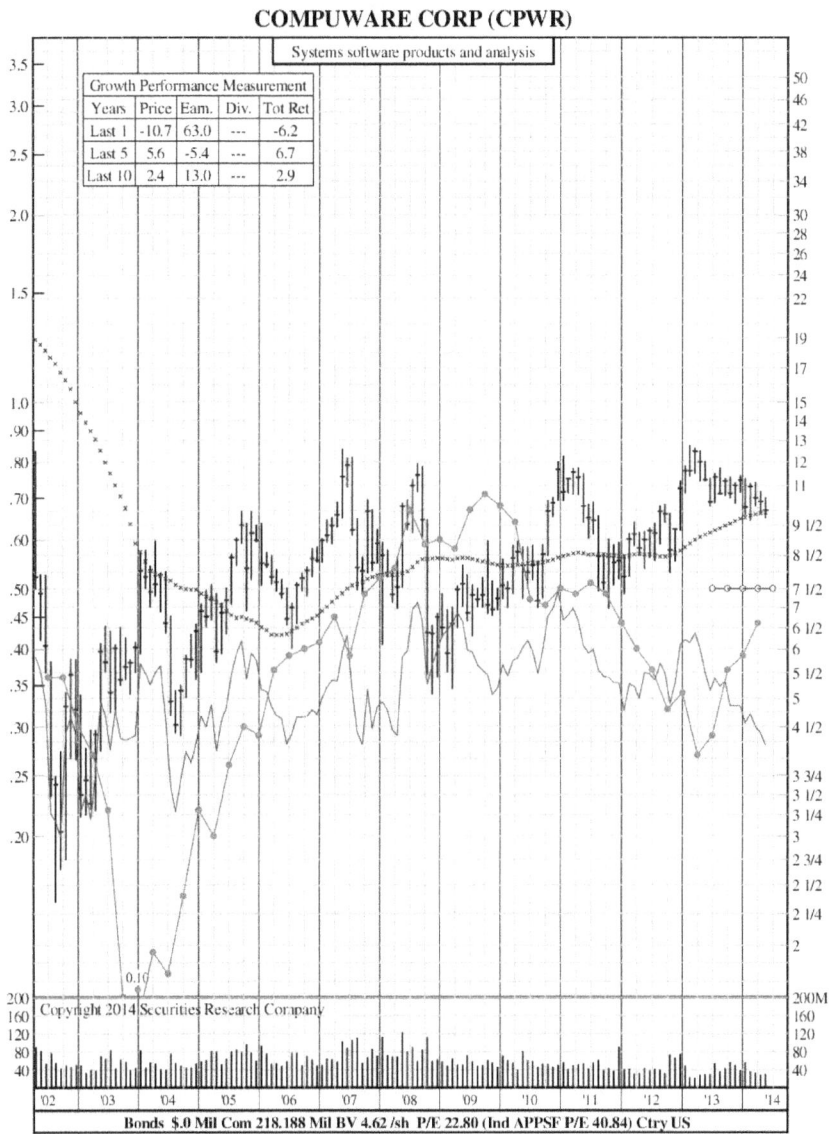

Source: Securities Research Company

Figure 11.2

Compuware Corp.

www.ingramcontent.com/pod-product-compliance
Lightning Source LLC
Chambersburg PA
CBHW051334170526
45166CB00002B/808